Orthodoxy and Islam
in the Middle East

T0164155

Orthodoxy and Islam in the Middle East

The Seventh to the Sixteenth Century

By Constantin A. Panchenko

Translated by Brittany Pheiffer Noble and
Samuel Noble

HOLY TRINITY PUBLICATIONS
Holy Trinity Seminary Press
Holy Trinity Monastery
Jordanville, New York

2021

Printed with the blessing of His Eminence,
Metropolitan Hilarion First Hierarch
of the Russian Orthodox Church Outside of Russia

———————————————

Orthodoxy and Islam in the Middle East:
The Seventh to the Sixteenth Century
© 2021 Holy Trinity Monastery

HOLY TRINITY
SEMINARY PRESS

An imprint of

HOLY TRINITY PUBLICATIONS
Holy Trinity Monastery
Jordanville, New York 13361-0036
www.holytrinitypublications.com

ISBN: 978-1-942699-33-0 (paperback)
ISBN: 978-1-942699-35-4 (ePub)
ISBN: 978-1-942699-36-1 (Mobipocket)

Library of Congress Control Number: 2020949696

Cover Images: "The seizure of Edessa in Syria by the
Byzantine army and the Arabic counterattack" Scan from
illuminated manuscript the Chronicle of John Skylitzes:
National Library, Madrid, Spain. Source: commons.wikimedia.org,
Cplakidas; MAP: Asia Minor Vintage Map by Sergey Kamshylin.
Source: stock.adobe.com.

I do not cry for the king of this world ... but I cry and weep for the believing people, for how the Almighty, holding the whole world in his palm, despised His flock and He forsook his people for their sins.

—Antiochus Strategos, 631

Eighteenth-century icon of the Aleppo School depicting the Seventh Ecumenical Council, the acts of which preserved the epistle of Patriarch Theodore of Jerusalem to the patriarchs of Alexandria and Antioch, justifying the veneration of relics and icons. The Arabic text in the center of the icon is taken from a history of the council and begins, "In the name of our Lord, God and Master Jesus Christ, one hundred and fifteen years after the Sixth Council, the Seventh Holy Council was held in Nicaea." The representatives of the three Eastern patriarchs are portrayed in the middle of the assembly, including the syncellus John and the abbot Thomas, who actively supported the council's decisions.

Contents

viii   *Contents*

Foreword

We are pleased to offer in this concise study a broad survey of the life of the Orthodox Christian communities in the Middle East from the emergence (advent) of Islam in the early seventh century through the following nine hundred years. For those of us living in the modern West, this will open up a world that to all practical purposes is unknown to us: a world where many forms of Christianity existed (and still exist) and where conflicts between different Islamic tribes and dynasties create a tableau of great complexity and many contrasts.

The diligent reader will learn of overt persecution and martyrdom of Orthodox believers at the hands of both Muslims and pagans, together with suffering at the hands of the Latin Crusaders. But they will also see that this was not their constant reality and that in perhaps equal measure times of peaceful coexistence prevailed. Further, beyond these polarities of persecution and peace, attention is given to changes in the physical environment and other calamities such as plague and earthquake that were to bring about lasting changes in the life of the Church. In this respect, for all of us now living in a time of worldwide epidemic, the sufferings that are recounted here should put our own in perspective. Through all of these events and in the light of the fragility of the life of so many who lived through them, we can see that it is all the more a testament to God's work in history that in our own time these communities still exist and flourish, perennially renewed by the life of Christ in His Church.

Through the kaleidoscope of this work the reader will gain a vision of some of the seminal tides of human history that shaped and continue to mold both the region of the Middle East and the wider world to which it ultimately belongs as the cradle of civilization. As such we hope it will shape the understanding not only of those engaged in formal academic studies but of a wider readership as well.

Holy Trinity Monastery, September 2020

The Arab Conquest: Christians
in the Caliphate

The seventh century, the time of the Arab conquests, was the most dramatic landmark in the history of the Christian East. Boundaries between civilizations that had remained immutable for seven centuries were swept away within nine years. The global crisis of Late Antique[1] civilization—depopulation, deurbanization, the decline of the economy and culture, exacerbated by epidemics of the plague, and natural disasters in the sixth century—predestined the Byzantine Empire's inability to resist the Arab invasion. Justinian's ambitious reign (527–565 AD) had undermined the empire's last strength. The short-lived success of the Persian conquests at the beginning of the seventh century exposed Byzantium's political and military weakness. The Persian occupation struck a powerful blow to Greco-Roman culture and the Christian Church, leading to the breakdown of the administrative and economic structures of the Middle East. In the confrontation with Persia, the empire completely exhausted its military and economic resources. The spiritual unity of the state was undermined by schism in the Church, the confrontation between Orthodoxy and Monophysitism,[2] and the two centuries of futile attempts to overcome it. The Aramaic and Coptic East, the stronghold of Monophysitism, was oppressed by the authority of the *basileus* in Constantinople. The emperor Heraclius's (575–641 AD) attempt to reconcile the warring confessions on the basis of a compromise Monothelete[3] dogma only worsened the situation, pushing part of the Orthodox away from the emperor. As a result, the Muslims who invaded Palestine did not meet any serious resistance from the army or the population. Arab troops first crossed the Byzantine frontier in late 633; then, by 639, they had already conquered Syria and stood at the edge of the Anatolian Plateau; and in 642, the Byzantine army left Egypt. Byzantium lost half its territory and lands inhabited by millions of Christians; their holy places and the most famous monasteries and patriarchal sees all came under Islamic rule.[4]

Heretics who were persecuted in Byzantium clearly preferred the authority of the Muslim caliphs, for whom all Christian confessions were equal. The Orthodox of the Middle East ("Melkites"[5]) perceived the Muslim conquest far more negatively, but they were not exposed to special persecution by Arab authorities. It should be added that when the Monothelete heresy dominated in Constantinople, the Orthodox of Syria and Palestine were also in opposition to the Byzantine emperor. First of all, one can speak of

Patriarch Sophronius of Jerusalem (d. 637), to whom later tradition attributes a key role in shaping Muslim–Christian relations in the Caliphate, including the apocryphal "Pact of 'Umar."[6]

It should be recalled that the Muslim doctrine of the era of the "rightly guided caliphs"[7] and Umayyads was still in its formative stage and was very different from the classical Islam known to us, which took its current form only toward the beginning of the ninth century. Accordingly, the real status of non-Muslims in the Caliphate of the seventh and eighth centuries may have been very different from the legal constructs developed by jurists of the 'Abbasid era (750–1258 AD). Nevertheless, even in its later, classical forms, the Muslim legal system had a relatively tolerant attitude toward "People of the Book" (Christians and Jews), as well as toward several other categories of non-Muslims. The Arabs gave their Christian subjects the status of *dhimmis*[8]—people under the protection of Islam. *Dhimmis* enjoyed freedom of religion and general internal autonomy in exchange for political loyalty and the payment of a poll tax, the *jizya* (in reality, the *jizya* was as a rule paid collectively on behalf of the residents of a village or quarter). Christian communities in the Caliphate were ruled by their own ecclesiastical hierarchies, which held many of the prerogatives of secular authorities, in particular the right to collect taxes, conduct trials of coreligionists, and make decisions with regard to marriage and matters of property.[9]

In the seventh and eighth centuries, Christians still made up the majority of the population in the lands of the Caliphate from Egypt to Iraq. At the same time, Islamization was a major concern for Christian communities. Islam, the religion of the victorious conquerors, had high prestige. Most often, Christians converted to Islam under the influence of social and economic pressure. The lower classes sought to get rid of the burden of the poll tax and wealthy people wanted to raise their status and succeed in society. Mixed marriages,[10] the children of whom according to sharia became Muslims, were one of the most significant factors in eroding Christian communities, especially during the first Islamic century. Other factors, including forcible conversion to Islam, extermination, and ethnic cleansing, were not typical for the era of the Caliphate. Birth rates among Muslims and Christians appear to have been comparable. In any case, at the beginning of the era of the Crusades (1096–1271 AD), Christians still accounted for about half the population in Syria and Egypt.[11]

Because of their level of education, some *dhimmis* managed to obtain a high social position in the Caliphate. Non-Muslims had a strong position in trade and finance, practically monopolized the practice of medicine, and almost completely filled the ranks of the lower and middle levels of the administrative apparatus. Christian, including Orthodox, doctors and administrators were of great importance at the caliph's court. Masterpieces of Arab architecture of the late seventh and early eighth centuries were created by Christian craftsmen according to Byzantine techniques. The Umayyad period (661–750 AD) is considered the last flowering of Hellenistic art in the Middle East.[12] The Russian Arabist N. A. Ivanov somewhat shockingly, but not without reason, described the Umayyad Caliphate as "an Eastern Christian society under the rule of Muslims."[13]

The Fading Inertia of Byzantine Culture in the Seventh and Eighth Centuries

The Arabs had no experience managing a developed urban society and gladly made use of the services of former Byzantine officials in their tax administration. Before the eighth century, bureaucratic documents in Syria and Egypt were written in Greek. Part of the non-Muslim elite was closely associated with the ruling circles of the Caliphate. It is noteworthy that in contrast to the obvious presence of Jews and converts from a Jewish milieu in the entourage of Muhammad and the rightly guided caliphs, it was Christians who played a significant role under the Umayyads.[14]

The governors (emirs) of provinces were almost completely independent. The caliph could change them, but he could not intervene in their affairs. This semi-autonomous status of the provinces ensured a maximal preservation of the traditional way of life and political stability. The system of tax collection and distribution of pay to soldiers were decentralized. The imperial center only received very little of the surplus revenue from the provinces. The old regional elites remained in place and the Arabs did not encroach on their authority, remaining content with collecting taxes.[15]

Archaeological research in Palestine and Jordan in recent decades gives a picture of almost universal Christian presence in the cities of the Middle East in the seventh and eighth centuries, with Byzantine traditions of urban development, crafts, daily life, and culture remaining intact. Ecclesiastical organization and other forms of self-government were preserved in Christian communities. Churches were built and renovated and were decorated with mosaics almost indistinguishable from their Byzantine counterparts. The Arab conquest itself hardly left a material trace, and archaeologists have not found any destruction or fires. Several churches in Transjordan were consecrated in the second half of the 630s, right in the middle of the Muslim invasion. According to archaeological findings, there were fifty-six churches in the territory of modern Jordan until the second half of the eighth century and sometimes longer. Moreover, eight of them were constructed or decorated with mosaics during the Umayyad period.[16]

The best preserved architectural monuments of Umayyad Christianity include Umm al-Jimal in northeastern Jordan where fourteen churches and two monasteries were active in the seventh century; two dozen churches and seven monasteries were close by. At the beginning of the seventh century, there were more than fifteen churches in Jerash (Gerasa), to which only one mosque was added in the Umayyad period. Many churches in northwest Jordan were rebuilt during the era of the Caliphate and continued to be used until the Mamluk era (1250–1517 AD). In the village of Samra near Jerash, the mosaics of three churches date back to the beginning of the eighth century. Hundreds of Christian funerary stelae with inscriptions in Greek and Aramaic have also survived. In Madaba, there are Greek inscriptions mentioning the bishops and construction activity up to 663. In Ramla, which was founded by Arab governors in 717 as the new capital of Palestine, the Christians built two churches.[17]

Archaeological data about the relative prosperity of Christians is supported by the testimonies of Western pilgrims who visited the Holy Land—the bishops Arculf (c. 680), Willibald (720s), and to some extent Bernard (860s). They describe the ornate Church of the Holy Sepulchre in Jerusalem, the golden lamps over the Lord's Tomb, the golden cross crowning the Edicule,[18] and the churches and monasteries in the various holy places of Palestine, including Bethany, Mamre, the Ascension Mount, and the place of the Baptism in the Jordan, where later pilgrims no longer noticed any traces of a Christian presence.[19]

Along with this, in the seventh and early eighth centuries, aspects of the decline of Middle Eastern Christian society are already noticeable. Many churches, monasteries, and villages—including seats of dioceses—ceased to exist, either after the devastating earthquake at the beginning of the seventh century or after the Persian or Arab invasion. In some cities, churches were abandoned or converted into mosques and commercial facilities. Thus, in Fahl (Pella), the capital of the Arab province of Palestine, the neglect of the churches contrasted with the prosperity of the rest of the city. The clearest features of degradation and extinction appeared along the borders of the desert. Under the Umayyads, population density plummeted in central Transjordan. Toward the end of the seventh century, villages in the Negev were abandoned, including Beersheba, Elusa, and Nessana, famous for its papyrus archives preserving Greek and Arabic documents, the last of which date to the 680s.[20]

The Early Umayyads: "Byzantium after Byzantium"

The situation of Middle Eastern Orthodoxy under Arab rule was determined by a complex combination of internal and external factors, including the development of Muslim doctrine, the relationships between the Melkites and Byzantium and between the Byzantium and the Caliphate, as well as the struggle between various ethnoreligious groups in the Caliphate for influence in the Muslim administration.

The Arab conquerors tolerated all Abrahamic religions and Christian confessions equally. This contributed to the cultural rise of the Copts and Syrians and the final formation of the non-Chalcedonian churches in Egypt and Syria, which had previously been persecuted by the Byzantine authorities. At the same time, all the resources of the conquered lands were directed to the needs of the Muslim community and the Orthodox Church lost state support. In the first couple of decades after the Arab conquest of Byzantium's eastern provinces, the Melkites of Syria and Egypt underwent a profound crisis. Church structures were in a state of almost complete collapse, with all three patriarchal thrones vacant.

The last Melkite patriarch of Alexandria, Peter, escaped from Egypt with the departing Byzantine troops. After Peter's death in 654, a successor was not elected for him. With the arrival of the Arabs, the Monophysite Copts retaliated for their long-term persecution by the Byzantine emperors. The Coptic patriarch Benjamin, who had long been hiding in the desert to escape persecution, solemnly returned to Alexandria. The Monophysites seized Orthodox churches and monasteries and some Egyptian Christian sects, including part of the Melkites, joined the Coptic Church. After the death of the last Melkite bishops, the remnant of the Orthodox community in Egypt was led by priests ordained in Syria who formally adhered to Monotheletism.[21]

In Palestine, the patriarchal throne was vacant after the death of Sophronius in the spring of 637. A significant proportion of the bishops rejected Monothelete dogma and tried to rely on the support of Rome, the last stronghold of Orthodoxy, which opposed Monothelete Constantinople. The Pope of Rome was appointed from among the Palestinian bishops locum tenentes for the patriarchal see, who ruled the Palestinian church for the next three decades.[22]

Continuity in the Patriarchate of Antioch was interrupted from approximately 609 to 611 and was not restored during the war with Persia, after which came the Monothelete troubles. In 639/640, however, Macedonius, a Monothelete, was ordained Patriarch of Antioch in Constantinople, but he and his successors tried to direct the affairs of the Church of Antioch from Byzantium without taking the risk of appearing in Arab-controlled territory. That segment of the Melkites of Syria who shared Monothelete dogma obeyed the patriarch of Antioch residing in Constantinople. Those who remained faithful to Orthodoxy acknowledged the supremacy of the locum tenens of the patriarchal see in Jerusalem.[23]

The coming of the Umayyad dynasty into power in the Caliphate in 661 was an important milestone in the political development of Muslim society, as it increasingly absorbed the heritage of the pre-Islamic empires of the region. The political center shifted from the oases of western Arabia to the zone of the urban civilization of the Fertile Crescent. Syria came to be the core of the state and the capital was transferred from Mecca to Damascus. The Islamic theocracy was transformed into an Arab monarchy based on the dominance of Arab tribes as a privileged military caste.

The first Umayyad caliph Mu'awiya (661–680) spent many years as governor of Syria before his accession to the throne. His time spent surrounded by Christians contributed to his broad religious tolerance. Middle Eastern Christian chroniclers preserved an exceptionally positive image of this ruler. Before assuming caliphal dignity, Mu'awiya had prayed at Golgotha and at the Tomb of the Theotokos in Jerusalem. The motives for these actions, which are contrary to the Muslim dogma denying the crucifixion and resurrection of Jesus, remain unclear, but it is evident that Mu'awiya sought to win the sympathy of Syrian Christians. In 679, at the expense of the treasury, he restored the Church of Edessa, which had been damaged by an earthquake (this unprecedented event remained, however, exceptional, even for Mu'awiya's politics). The Maronite Chronicle of the 660s recounts a religious dispute between Jacobites and Monotheletes in 659 in the presence of Mu'awiya, which testifies to his interest in Christian dogma.[24] A characteristic example of the cultural syncretism of early Umayyad society is a Greek inscription from 662 of the Christian administrator of the town of Hamat Gader, south of Lake Tiberias, about the reconstruction of the complex of thermal baths, which mentions the Caliph Mu'awiya (whose Arabic title, *amir al-mu'minin* is given in Greek letters) with an image of the cross accompanying the text.[25] It has been suggested in scholarly literature that in Mu'awiya's time the term *al-mu'minun* ("the believers") indicated followers of all monotheistic religions and that Mu'awiya regarded himself as head of the entire multiethnic and multi-faith population of the Caliphate. It was only later that the Arab state took on a markedly Islamic character.[26]

With the transfer of the political center of the state to Syria, the Arab rulers found themselves in a densely Christian environment. In Damascus, there formed an Orthodox center of influence, including a group of high-ranking Melkite officials who had a marked impact on the religious policy of the Caliphate. At the court of Mu'awiya several influential Christians were known, the most notable of whom was the Orthodox Sarjoun (Sergius) ibn Mansur, the caliph's secretary for Syria and manager of his personal finances.[27] In the absence of Melkite patriarchs, leadership of the community was assumed by the Orthodox secular elite, led by Sarjoun. Around 668, Mu'awiya restored the throne of the Melkite patriarchs in Jerusalem;[28] however, even after that, Sarjoun's influence at the caliph's court—and thus also in the Melkite community—remained unquestioned.

Hagiographic tradition says that Sarjoun ibn Mansur was the father of the greatest Christian theologian and writer John of Damascus (676–748), who bore the family name Mansur.[29] Sarjoun himself is also sometimes considered in the literature to be son of the semilegendary governor of Damascus Mansur, who handed the city over to the Arab commander Khalid ibn al-Walid in 636.[30] Although sources do not offer clear evidence of kinship between Mansur and Sarjoun, it is sufficiently obvious that within the Orthodox community (as well as in other Christian ethnoreligious groups in the Caliphate) a hereditary quasi-aristocracy had formed that occupied prominent positions in the civil administration and church hierarchy.

During the period of Monothelete dominance in the Byzantine Empire, the Orthodox of the Caliphate perceived the Byzantine emperors as heretics and the Arabs did not consider their Melkite subjects to be a Byzantine "fifth column." The Russian scholar Vasily Bartold already drew attention to the fact that despite Mu'awiya's frequent wars with Byzantium, the Middle Eastern Orthodox were not subject to any harassment.[31] However, the balance of power dramatically changed in 681 after the Sixth Ecumenical Council in Constantinople, when Monotheletism was anathematized and religious unity between Byzantium and the Orthodox of Syria and Egypt was restored. The defeated Monothelete creed suddenly took on new life in the land of the Caliphate. A significant proportion of the Middle Eastern Aramaean Melkites continued to adhere to this belief. The Syro-Lebanese Monothelete community developed into the Maronite subethnicity, receiving its name, according to one version, from the name of its first spiritual center, the Monastery of St Maroun on the Orontes or, in another version, from Yuhanna Maroun, the legendary founder of the Maronite church organization at the turn of the seventh to the eighth century. During this period, there were repeated clashes between the Orthodox and the Maronites in various areas of Syria and Lebanon. Polemic with Maronite doctrine became one of the areas of Melkite theology in the eighth and ninth centuries. Thanks to the Byzantine–Arab peace treaty of 685, the Orthodox were able to win the authorities of the Caliphate over to their side and to use them in the fight against Monotheletism. Relying on Arab military force, Sarjoun ibn Mansur brought about the submission of the Syrian heretics.[32] In 745, Patriarch of Antioch Theophylact bar Qanbar, who enjoyed the support of the caliph Marwan, once more attempted military action. According to some authors, in 745, after a wave of Melkite–Maronite conflicts at the Monastery of St Maroun, Aleppo, and Manbij, the Maronites created an autonomous church headed by a patriarch. It was only later that the mythologized historiography of that community granted the laurels of "founding father" to Yuhanna Maroun.[33]

Christians of various denominations actively fought for access to administrative positions to influence the caliphs. During the reign of the caliph ʿAbd al-Malik (685–705), a Monophysite group led by Athanasius bar Gumoye from Edessa played a prominent role in the state. The caliph made Athanasius tutor and secretary to his younger brother ʿAbd al-ʿAziz, the governor of Egypt. For two decades, Athanasius governed the richest province on his behalf, collecting taxes and amassing an enormous fortune. For obvious reasons, Sarjoun ibn Mansur could not get along with a rival of such stature. After the death of ʿAbd al-ʿAziz around 704, when Athanasius returned to his homeland with a huge caravan of property, Sarjoun remarked to the caliph,

"Bar Gumoye has ransacked all the cellars of Egypt."[34] 'Abd al-Malik contented himself with confiscating half of Athanasius's wealth.

Athanasius's example demonstrates the extent of the prosperity of the region's Christian elite at the courts of the emirs in the Caliphate's provinces. In Egypt, alongside influential Monophysites, Orthodox courtiers of 'Abd al-'Aziz are known to have received from him the right to build a church in Hulwan for their coreligionists.[35] Although the patriarchal throne of Alexandria continued to be vacant, toward the end of the seventh century an Orthodox ecclesiastical organization with its bishops was somehow reconstituted in Egypt. Egyptian Melkites participated in church life in Byzantium: at the Sixth Council the Patriarchate of Alexandria was represented by the priest Peter, who signed the conciliar acts with the title "Vicar of the Apostolic See." He also attended the Council in Trullo of 691 as a bishop.[36]

The Late Umayyads: Pressure Mounts

At the turn of the seventh to the eighth century, the internal structure of the Caliphate underwent important changes and the position of Christians at the caliphal court was shaken. ʿAbd al-Malik emerged the winner of a long civil war and started large-scale reforms to strengthen the Arab–Muslim state.

In 697, a land census was carried out (prior to this, earlier Byzantine or Persian land assessments had been used in the administration). Taxation was stepped up and was transferred to special administrative structures outside the control of the governors. Attempts were made to introduce individual taxation of *dhimmis*, which was received very painfully among Christians (prior to this, non-Muslim communities paid the poll tax collectively). In order to replace the "barbaric" imitations of Byzantine and Sasanian coinage,[37] which were in circulation in the Caliphate, with all their state and religious imagery, coins with Islamic symbols started to be minted in the 690s. Around the year 700, a reform of the

Arabic script was carried out and diacritics and vowel signs were introduced. This made it possible to write texts of any complexity, which contributed to the final canonization of the Qur'an and the translation of the state's record-keeping into Arabic (700–705), something that later Muslim authors portrayed as an attempt to put an end to the monopoly of Christian scribes, led by Sarjoun, in the administrative structures.[38] This change, however, did not much alter the status of *dhimmi* officials, who for the most part had mastered Arabic.

'Abd al-Malik's reforms, which entailed increasing the tax burden and every manner of control over the taxable population, provoked discontent among Christians and a surge of apocalyptic prophecies. Starting in the 720s, the Egyptian Copts, and in particular the inhabitants of the Nile Delta, repeatedly rebelled against the tax policy of the authorities.

'Abd al-Malik's son al-Walid I (705–715) was renowned for his large-scale construction projects. In the year 706 he confiscated the Cathedral of John the Baptist in Damascus from the Melkites and on its site the grandiose Umayyad Mosque was erected. It was designed to overshadow the beauty of the Christian churches with its splendor and became yet another symbol of the self-assertion of Arab–Muslim civilization.[39] In their own times, Mu'awiya and 'Abd al-Malik had also attempted to obtain the cathedral, but the Christian elites managed to fend them off by referring to the guarantee of the security of *dhimmis*' property given by Khalid ibn al-Walid when he captured Damascus. The new caliph, however, paid no attention to Khalid's decree. Similarly, during the construction of a mosque in Ramla, Muslims seized columns that had been prepared by the Christians of neighboring Lydda for one of its churches.[40]

The caliph ʿUmar II (717–720) was a figure who stood in sharp contrast to the other Umayyads. He led an ascetic way of life, in every way stressing his religious zeal and attempting to restore the ways of early Islam as imagined by conservative Muslim circles. The caliph abolished many taxes, increased salaries for troops, and encouraged *dhimmis* to convert to Islam, which caused the treasury's income to fall. The name of ʿUmar II is associated with the first religiously motivated persecution of unbelievers. ʿUmar introduced restrictions for Christians in dress, forbade the building of new churches, and encouraged *dhimmis* to convert to Islam. Muslim tradition attributes him with expelling Christian officials from service. Such "purges" of infidels from the administrative apparatus were carried out during each persecution. It did not, however, achieve tangible results because for a long time not enough educated Muslims in the Caliphate were able to replace Christians in public service.[41]

The series of anti-Christian measures undertaken by the subsequent caliph, Yezid II (720–724), who demanded that all images in churches be destroyed and pigs within the country be exterminated, were equally short-lived and ineffective.[42]

In this period, the Orthodox community was already led by Sarjoun's successors, including John of Damascus, who inherited from his father the post of caliphal secretary. According to one account, John's departure from government service and entrance into monasticism took place during the anti-Christian persecution of ʿUmar, who sought to remove Christians from the state bureaucracy.[43]

Soon, however, Arab–Melkite relations entered into a new, more favorable phase. When the doctrine of iconoclasm prevailed in Byzantium in 726, it provoked a sharp rejection from Middle Eastern Orthodox. It was here, in the late 720s and early 730s, that John of Damascus formulated the first profound justification for the veneration of icons, and Middle Eastern bishops anathematized the emperor Leo the Isaurian.[44] Byzantine monks, fleeing iconoclast persecution, came to Palestine. On the day of Pentecost 764, the three Eastern patriarchs, by prior agreement each in their own city, anathematized Bishop Cosmas of Epiphania (Hama), who had joined the iconoclasts.[45] The acts of the Seventh Ecumenical Council preserved the epistle of Patriarch Theodore of Jerusalem (d. after 767) to the patriarchs of Alexandria and Antioch, justifying the veneration of relics and icons. The Seventh Ecumenical Council in 787, which restored the veneration of icons, was attended by representatives of the three Eastern patriarchs, the syncellus John, and the abbot Thomas, who actively supported the council's decisions.[46]

From the beginning of the iconoclast turmoil, the Umayyad Caliph Hisham (724–742) no longer had any reason to see his Melkite subjects as supporters of Byzantium. This seems to be behind the restoration of the Orthodox patriarchal sees of Alexandria (731) and Antioch (742).[47]

Thus, by the middle of the eighth century, Orthodox ecclesiastical structures in the regions of Egypt and Syria were completely restored and mechanisms developed for the self-government of the Orthodox community, which upheld its interests before the Muslim authorities. The laity did not play as much of a role in the management of the community as it had during the era of Sarjoun and John of Damascus. In the Orthodox community during the eighth to tenth centuries, however, one can clearly observe a merger of the secular elite with the theocratic church hierarchy and the "migration" of influential laymen to bishops' posts. Sarjoun's adopted son Cosmas became bishop of Mayouma. In the ninth century, two descendants of Mansur held the See of Jerusalem: Sergius (844–860) and Elias (880–909). Influential physicians repeatedly became patriarchs of Alexandria, such as Politianus (767–801) and the famous historian Eutychius (Saʿid ibn Batriq, 934–940). Members of the class of *kuttab* (scribes) ascended to the throne of Antioch, such as Elias I (905–932/4), Theodosius II (935–942), and Christopher (960–967).[48]

Arab authorities repeatedly interfered in the election of patriarchs, seeking the election of their protégés and sometimes even Christian officials in the administration of the Caliphate who had not previously held any spiritual dignity. The Muslims were primarily concerned with ensuring the loyalty of the Melkite bishops. For this reason, the Syrian monk Stephen who did not know Greek and was in no way connected with Byzantium was made the first patriarch of Antioch in 742.[49]

The political sympathies of the Melkite bishops, balancing between the two empires, could differ quite a lot. On the one hand, around 757, Patriarch Theodore of Antioch (751–773) was exiled to Transjordan for alleged contacts with Byzantium.[50] On the other hand, some bishops cooperated with the Muslim authorities so long as it did not affect their religious beliefs. Patriarch Job of Antioch (811/2–842) went the furthest of all down that path. Around 821, by order of the caliph, he crowned the Byzantine rebel Thomas the Slav with the imperial diadem (for which he was excommunicated by the Synod of Constantinople), and in 838, he accompanied the Arab army in the campaign against Amorium and persuaded its besieged garrison to surrender.[51]

At the same time, for the majority of Melkites, even those absolutely loyal to the Muslims, there was a long-standing characteristic attitude toward Arab rule as something that God allowed to take place for the time being, a feeling of belonging to the Byzantine world, and the perception that the Emperor of Constantinople was their true lord and protector.

The Culture of the Melkites

In the seventh and eighth centuries, the cultural creativity of the Syro-Palestinian Christians continued. The eastern half of the Byzantine Empire that had been captured by the Arabs was still part of a common cultural space with the rest of Byzantium. The contribution of the Middle Eastern Melkites to general Byzantine culture was comparable to what was created within the empire itself.

Mosaics of Palestinian and Transjordanian churches of the eighth century represent rare examples of Byzantine fine art contemporary to the iconoclastic era, which did not leave similar monuments in Byzantium.

The Sinaite monks John Climacus (d. c. 650) and Anastasius of Sinai (d. c. 700) had a tremendous impact on Eastern Christian theology. Andrew of Crete (660–740), the great composer of Byzantine church poetry, spent the first half of his life in the Middle East and was a monk of Mar Saba (the Lavra of St Sabbas the Sanctified) and secretary to the *locum tenens* of the See of Jerusalem. There, at Mar Saba and in

Jerusalem, John of Damascus (c. 675–749 AD), the greatest Christian thinker of the eighth century and the last of the fathers of the church, spent the most productive years in his life. It is thought that John of Damascus' efforts to codify Orthodox belief were motivated by the Melkite community's need for self-affirmation in the context of the cultural and political reality of the Caliphate and the ideological challenges posed by rival Christian confessions, Judaism, Manicheism, and Islam, which during these years underwent an analogous period of systematization of religious beliefs.[52]

The Damascene's foster brother, Cosmas of Mayouma, also a monk of Mar Saba and then bishop of Mayouma (near Gaza), left an enormous poetic heritage. Living at the turn of the eighth to the ninth century, the Sabaite monks Stephen the Younger and Leontius composed a number of hagiographical works about the Palestinian martyrs and ascetics of their time.

The chronicles of Syrian Melkites had a direct influence on the development of Byzantine historiography. The anonymous Melkite chronicle of 780 was extensively used by Theophanes the Confessor in his *Chronography*.[53] In contrast to the self-contained, sealed-off classical culture of Byzantium, the Melkites, who lived at the crossroads of civilizations, were more open to cultural contacts. This resulted in both their polemics with people of other faiths and their translating into Greek works of Syriac literature.

Although most of the Orthodox of the Holy Land were not Greeks, but rather Hellenized Aramaeans, as well as Arabs in Transjordan and the Negev, the language of

Christian literature was predominantly Greek. The liturgy was conducted in Greek with Syriac translation, when necessary. Within the Patriarchate of Antioch, liturgical services were conducted in Syriac and Orthodox literature existed in Syriac. It included not only liturgical texts and translations from Greek but also original works. Mention can be made of the anti-Monophysite treatises of George, bishop of Martyropolis, and his disciples Constantine and Leo, who successively held the episcopal see of Harran at the end of the seventh and beginning of the eighth centuries or the anonymous Aramaic *Life of the Sixty New Martyrs of Jerusalem* composed in the middle of the eighth century.[54]

The theme of suffering for the faith held a special place in the literature and consciousness of the Caliphate's Christians. Images of the martyrs were important symbols of identity. The history of the churches of Antioch and Jerusalem in the eighth and early ninth centuries was adorned by the deeds of several such martyrs. Acquaintance with their biographies paradoxically confirms the relative tolerance of Muslim authorities and their compliance with the rules of sharia regarding *dhimmis*. Many of the Christians executed by the Arabs were Byzantine prisoners of war who did not belong to the category of *dhimmis*, such as the Sixty New Martyrs of Jerusalem in 724, the Forty Martyrs of Amorium in 845, or the Byzantine monk Romanos the New (d. 778), who moreover was charged with espionage.[55] Some of the zealots wanting to be found worthy of a martyr's crown themselves publicly denounced the Islamic faith and the "false prophet" Muhammad, which, of course, was severely punished according to Muslim law (Peter, metropolitan of Damascus, who, however, was not executed but rather exiled in 743, and Peter of Capitolias, murdered in 744).[56] Islam punished apostasy just as radically: executed for this were Christopher, a monk of Mar Saba and a convert from Islam in 799 or 805, and St Anthony/Rawh, a Muslim noble who converted to Christianity and tried to win over others. On account of the same slanderous accusation, Elias the New from Baalbek was martyred either in 779 or, according to a different estimate, in 795.[57]

Among the martyrs of the early Arab period is the interesting figure 'Abd al-Masih al-Najrani al-Ghassani (d. in the 860s or, according to another account, the 750s). A Christian who converted to Islam and took part in the raids on Byzantium, he repented of his past, returning to Christianity and becoming a monk on Sinai. Desiring to die for Christ like other voluntary martyrs, 'Abd al-Masih went to Ramla to denounce Islam before the Arab governor. At the last moment, however, the monk did not have sufficient strength of will and he left the city. Human weakness, no stranger to 'Abd al-Masih and something that the author of his *Life* does not attempt to hide, distinguishes this figure from the stereotyped hagiographic heroes abundantly represented in Byzantine literature. In the end, the monk nevertheless acquired a martyr's crown when one of the Muslims recognized him and accused him of apostasy.[58]

These examples show the high intensity of religious feeling among Middle Eastern Melkites in the seventh and eighth centuries. The same can be said for the monastic movement, not much inferior to that of the Early Byzantine era. Stories about the Sinaite fathers—contemporaries of John Climacus—suggest that the early Byzantine monastic tradition was maintained unchanged.[59] On the basis of the written sources, the total number of Palestinian monasteries was quite large, but a precise count cannot be given. Alongside the monasteries in cities and densely populated rural areas, the remote monasteries of the Judean Desert and the Jordan Valley attracted the attention of pilgrims and hagiographers. Central among these was Mar Saba, about 15 kilometers to the east of Jerusalem. Along with Mar Saba should be mentioned the lavras of St Euthymius the Great, St Theodosius the Great, St Chariton (Mar Kharitun), and others along the same mountain range between Jerusalem and the Dead Sea. Among the monasteries along the Jordan, the best known were the Monastery of St John the Baptist, where at the beginning of the eighth century there were as many as twenty monks,[60] the Monastery of St Gerasimus, and the Monastery of St George of Koziba in the Wadi Qelt. Among the monks of the Judean Desert mentioned in the sources are natives of Palestine, Transjordan, Egypt, and southern Syria. Syriac-speaking monks had a separate community with its own presbyter in Mar Saba. The abundance of Georgian translations of Arabic and Syriac hagiographical texts of Palestinian origin dating from the eighth to tenth centuries implies the presence of Georgian monks in the Judean Desert.

The main source for the history of Palestinian monasticism in the eighth century is the *Life* of the famous ascetic,

Stephen the Wonderworker the Elder (725–794), written by his disciple Leontius at the beginning of the ninth century.

In his youth, Stephen spent five years in a narrow cave, almost never leaving it. Several times for the entirety of Lent the hermit went into the desert near the Dead Sea, where he fed only on the tips of reeds. During the last thirty years of his life, he received the gifts of conversing with God, healing the sick, and predicting the future. There were monks who claimed to have seen Stephen walking on the water of the Jordan and the Dead Sea with his hands lifted up to heaven, glowing radiantly. An interesting event in Stephen's life is a conversation he had with a Christian from Transjordan, whom the ascetic encouraged to become a monk and go out into the desert. "Now it is possible for people to please God in the world as well as in the desert," Stephen's companion replied to him.

> It seems preferable to me to suffer evil with God's people who are in great distress and affliction … than to pay attention to oneself in silence and not help anyone … Now life in the world is more difficult and sorrowful … for we see that monks enjoy great tranquility and rest, while those in the world are in great distress and misfortune.[61]

Perhaps the person saying this was unwittingly exaggerating, but nevertheless the perception among laypeople in the Caliphate of the monastic life as quiet and comfortable is quite remarkable.

At the same time, relations within the monastic community were not always sunny. There are mentions of conflicts in Mar Saba. According to the hagiographer of St Stephen the Wonderworker, "Some novices, deceived by demons, rebelled at the end of the service and beat some of the elders with sticks and maliciously laid hands on the venerable … abbot himself."[62]

There is significantly less information about Syriac monasticism. Its main center, as during the Byzantine period, remained the Monastery of St Symeon the Stylite (Mar Sam'an) in the desert 70 kilometers northwest of Aleppo.

The ʿAbbasid Revolution

The most important internal milestone in the history of the Caliphate was the coming to power of the ʿAbbasid dynasty in 750 after a bitter civil war. Egypt briefly became the last refuge of the defeated Umayyads. Taking advantage of the collapse of power structures, the local Christians started a revolt.

The insurrection was primarily caused by economic oppression by the Arab governors. After ʿAbd al-Malik's reforms, officials became more exacting with regard to tax collection. Peasants were prevented from migrating or attempting to take shelter from taxation in monasteries. Christian grassroots administration was replaced by Muslim governors. The authorities imposed civil servants who were responsible for collecting taxes. The fiscal apparatus became more efficient, and so oppression of Coptic peasants increased. In response, starting in 725, the Christians repeatedly rebelled.[63] These uprisings were not religious in nature and the Church, concerned about preserving its privileges and property, did not try to lead the popular unrest. Nevertheless, in 750 both patriarchs—Coptic and Orthodox—joined the revolt. In one of the battles, the patriarchs were captured, but the Orthodox primate Cosmas managed to get ransomed. Finally, 'Abbasid troops invaded Egypt and defeated the Umayyads.[64]

Under the new dynasty, the political center of the state moved from Damascus to Mesopotamia. The displacement of trade routes and centers of economic activity painfully affected the well-being of Middle Eastern Christians. Unlike under the Umayyads, Melkites did not play a serious role at the 'Abbasid court. Among the Christian denominations in Baghdad, the Nestorians were dominant. In 912, they foiled an attempt by the Melkites to gain a foothold in the 'Abbasid capital, achieving the expulsion of the Orthodox metropolitan of Baghdad. Among the heads of all the Christian churches, only the Nestorian catholicos was allowed to have a residence in the Caliphate's capital.[65]

With the coming to power of the 'Abbasids, the moral climate in the government changed and many Muslim caliphs attempted to demonstrate their piety, which adversely affected the position of peoples of other faiths. Contrary to the previous caliphs' tendency to patronize the Melkites during their conflicts with heretical Byzantine emperors, the greatest of the 'Abbasid caliphs, al-Mansur (755–775) severely persecuted Orthodox Christians in his domains at the same time as the iconoclast persecution under the emperor Constantine V Copronymus (743–775) in Byzantium. The death of the two monarchs, which occurred in the same year, was welcomed in the Melkite Chronicle: "These two terrible beasts, who for so long had plagued the human race with equal ferocity, died by God's merciful providence."[66]

Generally speaking, under the early 'Abbasids, persecution broke out only sporadically. The caliph al-Mahdi (775–783) demanded that the last Bedouin Christians from the tribe of Tanukh in northern Syria convert to Islam. Their leader refused and was executed. The Tanukhid women, however, retained their religion, and churches were active in the tribe's territory for some time. Several Christians were martyred in Emesa (Homs) in 780. In 807, many churches in Syria were destroyed at the order of Harun al-Rashid.[67] In general, the position of Middle Eastern Christians did not depend so much on the policies of the caliphs as on the mood of the governors, some of whom subjected Christians to extortion and destroyed their churches, whereas others allowed them to renovate their places of worship and to erect new ones.[68]

The First Crisis of the Christian East

S tarting in the middle of the eighth century, there was an increasing number of crises in the life of Middle Eastern Melkites. The catastrophic earthquake in January 749 led to the destruction of many cities and monasteries that were never restored. Inhabitants abandoned Gerasa, Gadara, Umm al-Jimal, and other cities. A number of villages were simply abandoned but not destroyed.

At the same time, hundreds of towns and villages on the rocky hills between Apamea and Aleppo, in the region archaeologists call "the country of the dead cities," were abandoned. These cities had once thrived on account of the export of olive oil through Antioch to all corners of the Pax Romana. The rupture of old ties and the decline of Antioch forced farmers to abandon the highly specialized economy of olive cultivation and to return to subsistence farming. Wheat could not grow in the arid hills and residents left their homes to go down into the valleys.[69]

From the beginning of the ʿAbbasid era, church construction declined, the quality of mosaics decreased, and the
language of inscriptions deteriorated; thus, local Christians
lost their knowledge of Greek.[70] The traces of iconoclastic
damage, discovered in many Jordanian churches, also have
been associated by historians with this period of time. No
doubt, the Christians themselves destroyed images of living
creatures, sometimes carefully replacing them with new
mosaics. In the most famous of these mosaics, the image of
a bull was removed and replaced with an inanimate date
palm. In this case, because of the negligence of the workmen,
hooves and a tail hang from the bottom of the palm trunk.
The motivations for these acts are rather vague, but it seems
that those who vandalized the mosaics were not inspired
by the theories of the Byzantine iconoclasts, but rather by
Islamic (or a broader Semitic?) rejection of images of living
beings. Clearly, there was either pressure on Christians from
the Muslim environment or major shifts in the attitudes of
these Christians during the ʿAbbasid era.[71]

By the turn of the eighth to the ninth century original
literary activity by Christians almost ceased, writers and
saints disappeared, and Greek fell into disuse. Both literary
and material sources themselves, by which we can judge the
subsequent life of Middle Eastern Christians, disappeared
or radically changed. Joseph Nasrallah called the three hundred years from the ninth to the eleventh centuries the "great
lacuna" in the history of Palestinian monasticism.[72] These
words can be applied to almost the entirety of the Orthodox
Middle East during the High Middle Ages.

It can be argued with reasonable certainty that the crisis in Middle Eastern Christian society did not occur immediately following the earthquake of 749, although the latter did deal a severe blow to the ecclesiastical and secular structures of the Melkite community. There are several examples of construction activity by Christians of Transjordan in the second half of the eighth century. Archaeologists have discovered inscriptions marking the renovation of churches in Umm al-Rasas in 756 and Madaba in 767.[73] By the end of the eighth century, however, such activities came to naught.

The decline of the Christian community was compounded by the general political instability of the Caliphate and the inability of authorities to maintain order and stability. The most striking evidence of this kind is the narrative of Stephen the Sabaite concerning the martyrdom of Sinaite monks killed by the Saracens in 796. It gives a vivid picture of the bloody chaos in Palestine at the end of the eighth century when the Bedouin tribes of Mudar and Yemeni fought each other. Many villages were looted and burned, whereas the villagers discarded everything and fled to the cities, which, however, were not much of a safe haven. Hordes of bandits ravaged Gaza, Ashkelon, and Eleutheropolis. In this situation, the monks of the Lavra of St Sabbas "fearing what is human" made the decision neither to seek salvation beyond the walls of the Holy City nor to leave the monastery, which otherwise might have been destroyed by nomads and would have ceased to exist as an ancient center of monastic struggle. In March of 797, a group of bandits broke into the lavra and tortured the Sabaites, demanding that they tell them the whereabouts of the monastery's treasures. Eighteen monks were suffocated by smoke in one of the caves and two others died from wounds. Their death was extolled by the hagiographer Stephen the Sabaite, an eyewitness to the event, who compared the monks of the lavra to the ancient martyrs, stressing that they died "not for a stone or a tree" but in the name of Christ.[74]

The crisis of Palestinian monasticism was largely associated with the rampaging nomadic element in the Judean hills and multiple devastations of the monasteries at the turn of the eighth to the ninth century. Although the monks said with fervor that they should not "fear those who kill the body, but are unable to kill the soul,"[75] the common human instinct for self-preservation was not alien to them. Even contemporaries, who believed that Stephen the Wonderworker was the last of the great ascetics, felt the nascent decline of the monastic movement. "At the present time," wrote Leontius, Stephen's biographer, "monastic struggle has weakened in the ten years since the earthquake [of 749?] and it will grow weaker and weaker because laziness and carelessness will increase."[76]

Sinaite monasticism entered a period of decline at the same time as Palestinian monasticism. In the Early Arab period, almost all the cells and monasteries on Mount Horeb, towering over the Sinai Monastery of the Burning Bush (St Catherine's), were abandoned. Medieval ceramics have been found at only three of fifteen sites from the Byzantine period. The monasteries in the Umm Shomer mountains to the south of Mount Sinai likewise went derelict. Traces of a later presence are found only in four of the eleven Byzantine monasteries. The very quality of the construction of churches and cells deteriorated sharply—the rectangular Byzantine buildings of hewn stone were replaced by rougher structures with rounded corners built of unhewn stones.[77]

Disasters occurred repeatedly for Palestinian Christians in 809 and 813, during the civil war that engulfed the Caliphate after the death of Harun al-Rashid. According to the Byzantine chronicler Theophanes, the Hagarenes "killed, plundered and rampaged in every possible way and indiscriminately against each other and against the Christians," devastating the churches of the Holy City and the desert monasteries. The chronicler tells us of the arrival in Cyprus in 813 of many Christian refugees because in Syria, Egypt, and Africa there arose total anarchy, murders, robberies, and fornications in the villages and towns. In the Holy City they desecrated the most revered sites of the holy Resurrection. In the desert the famous lavras of St Chariton and St Sabbas (Mar Saba) and other monasteries and churches were likewise devastated.[78]

It was perhaps during these migrations that the last bearers of the Greek language and Byzantine literary culture left the Middle East.

During almost the same decade, the Coptic community experienced a similar political collapse. Starting in the eighth century, the population growth that was observed in Egypt during the first decades after the Arab conquest stopped. As mentioned, there were repeated uprisings of Coptic peasants against the tax burden, in which Muslims also sometimes took part. The most powerful uprising occurred in the years 829–831 in the Lower Delta. The last stronghold of the rebellious Copts' resistance to the caliph's army was the Bashmur district in the Lower Delta, the only location in Egypt convenient for guerrilla warfare and protected from external intrusions by nature itself. The Coptic patriarch, understanding the imbalance of forces, wrote to the rebels urging them to surrender to avoid a massacre. The church, which held a relatively privileged position, was loyal to the authorities since it depended on the state protection of its properties and was responsible for the conduct of its flock. The hierarchs did not attempt to take charge of the peasant uprisings or imbue them with the character of a "national" resistance; the church preached humility. Upon the arrival of the caliph al-Ma'mun in Egypt in February of 832, the patriarch Joseph, along with his Syrian Monophysite counterpart Dionysius and some bishops, was sent to negotiate with the leaders of the rebellion to force them to lay down their weapons. Reconciliation, however, was not achieved and hostilities resumed. The rebellion was crushed. Many churches and villages were burned down. Prisoners were executed and their families sold into slavery. Ethnic cleansing was carried out in Bashmur, where the surviving residents were sent to Iraq and the empty villages populated with Muslims. After this, the Copts no longer attempted to rebel.[79] According to several scholars, the suppression of the last Coptic peasant uprising "broke the back of mass adherence of Copts to Christianity."[80]

Attempts to explain the decline of Christianity in the Middle East by the fact of the Arab conquest have now been dismissed by scholarship in view of the clear evidence of the dynamic development of Christian communities in the seventh and eighth centuries. Epidemics, earthquakes, and the transfer of the Caliphate's capital to Baghdad, as well as an environmental crisis in the Middle East with desert encroachment and the expansion of nomadic tribes, undoubtedly played a negative role in the fate of Eastern Christians. However, according to scholars, all this is secondary. Something broke within the Christian community, but we are unable to grasp what this something was.[81] There appeared some deep and global laws of historical development, a process of losing vital energy that led to the death of the Classical civilization itself in whose bosom Christianity arose. The economic system, the culture, and the social relations characteristic of the Late Antique society disintegrated.

This process has been blurred over time, but if one is to choose an approximate date, it would be the civil war between al-Amin and al-Ma'mun in the years 811–813. It seems to have been perceived by contemporaries as a global catastrophe. The political upheavals caused a surge in apocalyptic feelings among Syriac Christians and the circulation of corresponding literature.[82] All this is not without profound symbolism: for them, the end of the world really did come. It was the end of a Middle Eastern society of the "Byzantine character," as we might call it.

The Dark Ages

The Birth of New Ethnic Groups
(Ninth to Eleventh Centuries)

Out of the darkness of the ninth century emerged a new society of Syro-Palestinian Christians, characterized by increasing Arabization and the loss of contact with Byzantine culture. The language barrier heightened the cultural isolation of the Middle Eastern Melkites from Byzantium. Greek authors of the mid-ninth to eleventh centuries write almost nothing about the Holy Land. Melkite Palestinian sources are few and particular. This vexing lack of sources indicates more eloquently than any texts the drastic drop in the educational level of the general population and the decay of old mechanisms of cultural reproduction. Likewise, almost no archaeological sites survive from this era. All this determined the extremely limited availability of information about the Melkite community in the 'Abbasid era.

More recently, however, scholars have managed to pull back the curtain on the history of Palestinian monasticism in the generation after Harun al-Rashid. The recently published paterikon of the Lavra of Mar Chariton preserves information about the flourishing monastic movement of the second third of the ninth century.[83] This is also evidenced by the literary activity of the monks of the Palestinian monasteries of the ninth and tenth centuries. It seems that the shock of the early ninth century was not as catastrophic as previously thought and the monasteries of the Judean Desert were able to recover.

There is reason to believe that the Middle Eastern Orthodox society of a "Byzantine character," which lingered in the Holy Land in the seventh and eighth centuries, disappeared and was replaced by a qualitatively different organism, a different identity. Not only the language changed but also social customs, the economy, and the type of settlement. The Christians' very habitat shrank as they left many parts of Transjordan, Hawran, Upper Mesopotamia, and Southern Palestine. The Melkites of the ninth and tenth centuries, unlike their ancestors, saw themselves as not so much a part of the Byzantine world as of the Arab world.

It is axiomatic that such processes should require a change in attitude and cultural outlook. During this era, Melkite scribes undertook a massive translation of Christian texts into Arabic, trying to create a civilized basis for young people and to restore cultural continuity. The bishop of Harran Theodore Abu Qurra (750–825/830) deserves the title "father of the nation" for Orthodox Arabs.

He was the first to write theological and apologetic treatises in Arabic, formulating a new identity for his community.

It appears that simultaneous to Arabization, the Melkites must have undergone a process of archaization of their social life, the revival of tribal relations in a Christian context. In the context of the Caliphate's growing weakness and the pressure from the nomadic periphery on the fellahin (agricultural workers) in the countryside, they had to find some means of collective survival. Even in cities where security was greater and the authorities were more capable, the population crept into religiously homogenous quarters. Each represented an ethnocultural reservation, walled with gates. Within them there were markets, baths, institutions of self-governance, and quasi-illicit structures of self-defense. In Baghdad, a system of homogenous quarters formed during a period of political unrest in the tenth century, while in Jerusalem, sources note this as happening during the second half of the eleventh century.[84] In Damascus, a similar transformation occurred between the 'Abbasid revolution and the Burid era (twelfth century).[85] It is not possible to give a more precise date because of the glaring lack of sources.

This is to say, once more, that almost everything changed for the Melkites apart from their religion. Their social degradation was not a unique phenomenon and similar processes took place during those centuries in other lands of the Christian East as well as within the Byzantine Empire itself. The Byzantium of Justinian and the Byzantium of the Macedonian dynasty are two completely different countries bound only by the cultural continuity of the state. Byzantium of the ninth and tenth centuries looks much more primitive than the Eastern Roman Empire of the fourth to sixth centuries, although with no less vitality. A similar deep social degeneration took place in early medieval Armenia. There, during its "Dark Ages" of the seventh to ninth centuries, even the construction of new churches was halted.

The geographically closest example to the Melkites is that of the Copts. We have mentioned the demographic stagnation in Egypt and the permanent "flight from the villages." During the ninth century, between half and two-thirds of agricultural land in the Nile Valley went uncultivated. On the border between the desert and arable land, Bedouin tribes appeared. Although they were few in numbers, as in Palestine, they represented a significant threat to the agricultural population. It was quite symptomatic that it was exactly from the ninth century that Coptic monks in the desert monasteries began to build fortified towers in their monasteries where they could hide supplies and themselves during attacks by nomads.[86]

After a century of instability and rebellions, the church organization, despite its outward conformism and loyalty to the Caliphate, was seriously damaged. According to archaeologists, from the early eighth century to the early ninth century, many small churches in the countryside dedicated to local Coptic saints disappeared or perhaps were destroyed. They were replaced by larger but numerically fewer churches associated with the basic figures of Christian worship, especially St George. The destruction of churches and the decline in the number of priests show the decay of the old rural communities. The Coptic population was deprived of its roots and lost touch with its "soil," which had been its main source of strength under the Byzantines. The way was cleared for the sacred landscape to be filled anew in the late Middle Ages with the tombs of local Muslim saints.[87]

In Egypt, there was a significant Muslim population in the cities starting in the ninth century. The pace of demographic change was increasing. Muslims went from being a minority to being a majority in Iran about 800 and in Syria and Egypt about 900.[88]

Arabization

The Arabic language spread among the Christians of the Middle East, displacing Greek and Syriac and necessitating the translation of Holy Scripture, liturgical texts, and the whole literary heritage of Christian civilization into Arabic. This process first began in Palestine, where traditionally worship in Greek and Syriac had coexisted and the translation of the services into a new language did not pose any problem psychologically.

The work of translating Christian literature into Arabic took place primarily in the monasteries of Southern Palestine: Mar Saba and the Lavra of St Chariton, as well as the Sinai Monastery of the Burning Bush. Translations of the Holy Scriptures, as well as of patristic and ascetic literature, were made from both Greek and Syriac. It is believed that the earliest translations date back to the 740s, and by the turn of the ninth century, Arabic Christian literature was already an established phenomenon.[89]

Over the next two and a half centuries, the number of Christian texts in Arabic increased rapidly. About sixty manuscripts have been preserved from the ninth to tenth centuries written in the so-called Old South Palestinian dialect.

Ninety percent of them are translations of the books needed for everyday church life: texts of the Holy Scriptures, homilies, hagiography, and patristic literature.[90] Along with this, there are original works that are partly hagiographical in character, partly apologetic, and polemical (five or six items). Their authors sought to prove the orthodoxy of their community in the face of the historical challenge posed by Islam and rival Christian confessions. The cult of Orthodox saints and martyrs, related in one way or another to Jerusalem and to Mar Saba (the Lavra of St Sabbas the Sanctified) as the sacred centers of Middle Eastern Christianity, also must have given spiritual support to the Melkite community in a non-Christian environment.

The first Orthodox author to begin writing in Arabic was the aforementioned native of Edessa, Theodore Abu Qurra, a bishop of Harran. He left several dozen theological treatises in different languages—his native Syriac, Greek, and Arabic, which was beginning to dominate the Middle East. In his writings, Theodore expounded and defended Orthodox dogmas, including the then-burning issue of the veneration of icons. Many works of Abu Qurra were translated into Greek and Georgian during the Middle Ages. Among Theodore's translators was a monk of Mar Saba by the name of Michael (761–846), who would later be syncellus of Patriarch Thomas of Jerusalem. Around 810, Michael composed a manual of Greek grammar and syntax, intended for the Palestinian monks studying Greek as a foreign language. It was part of that same intellectual endeavor of translating the Christian spiritual heritage into Arabic.[91]

In the ninth century, Christian scribes in Baghdad also started to write in Arabic. By the middle of the tenth century, the literary Arabic language was in universal use among the Orthodox of Syria and Egypt. By the late tenth century, Arabic had spread into the Coptic milieu.

Among the earliest classical writers of Arabic Christian literature, apart from Abu Qurra, we can name the scientist and encyclopedist Qusta ibn Luqa from Baalbek (830–912) and the prominent chroniclers Eutychius (Saʿid ibn Batriq), patriarch of Alexandria (876–940), and Agapius of Manbij (d. after 942).[92] The "cultural capital" of Melkites in the Caliphate was Mar Saba (or, more widely, the whole region of Southern Palestine), which developed its own school of Arabic Christian theology and even its own distinctive hand among the scribes who wrote so many of the extant Arabic Melkite manuscripts.[93]

The "Orientalization" of the Melkite community is also reflected in its perception of history. Characteristically, the chronicler Eutychius of Alexandria mentions almost nothing about the iconoclast upheavals of the eighth and ninth centuries. The last event in Byzantine church history that is well known to him is the Sixth Ecumenical Council in 681. From the middle of the eighth century, Eutychius stops giving information about the patriarchs of Constantinople (which by that time was already inaccurate). He wrote:

> I have not obtained the names of the patriarchs of Constantinople after the death of Theodore [Eutychius dates him to 773, but such a patriarch is unknown at this time] until the time that I wrote this book, as well

as the patriarchs of Rome from the time of Agapius [i.e., the Sixth Ecumenical Council of 681] ... the names of its patriarchs and information about them have not reached me.[94]

In Orthodox chronicles written in the Middle East in the tenth century, Muslim history and Muslim–Christian relations in the Caliphate increasingly displace information about the internal affairs of Byzantium.[95]

Links between the Orthodox of different provinces of the Caliphate were not weakened. In the lives of Palestinian ascetics of the eighth and ninth centuries, there is constant reference to monks of Syrian, Egyptian, and Mesopotamian origin leading an ascetic life in the monasteries by the Jordan. People of Syrian origin repeatedly became patriarchs of Alexandria. At the same time, Egyptian Melkites sometimes jealously guarded their independence from neighboring patriarchal sees, for example, in 907 making the newly arrived Patriarch of Alexandria Christodoulos (a native of Aleppo), who had been consecrated in Jerusalem, once again undergo the rite of consecration in Alexandria.[96] Patriarch Thomas (807–821) oversaw the reconstruction of the Church of the Holy Sepulchre at the expense of the wealthy Egyptian Christian Macarius, who may have been a Monophysite by confession.[97] Georgian monks had continued to live in the monasteries of the Middle East since Byzantine times. Many works of Syriac and Arabic literature from the early Middle Ages are preserved only in Georgian translation.[98] There are some indications suggesting that the greatest authority among the three Middle Eastern Orthodox patriarchs was enjoyed by the patriarch of Antioch, as he had the largest flock and most extensive territory. At the beginning of the ninth century, it was the Antiochian primate who tried to confirm his metropolitan in the capital of the Caliphate.[99]

Despite the Palestinian Christian community's isolation from Byzantium and the West, some ecclesiastical relationships were maintained as pilgrims continued to come to the Holy Land as they previously had. Toward the beginning of the ninth century, the Frankish emperor Charlemagne's Middle Eastern policy began to intensify. Although medieval chroniclers and Western historians of the nineteenth century exaggerated the scope of Frankish–Arab diplomatic contacts and the degree of Latin influence in the Holy Land, contacts between Aachen and Jerusalem undoubtedly existed. Frankish alms came to the Holy Sepulchre, and in the beginning of the ninth century in Palestine, a community of Latin monks was in continuous residence.[100] The Western pilgrim Bernard, who visited Jerusalem in 867, stayed there in a hostel for pilgrims from Western Europe founded by Charlemagne.[101] In the years 808–809, the dogmatic innovations of the Frankish monks living in Jerusalem, who added the *filioque* to the Creed, drew strong opposition from the monks of Mar Saba. The Latins appealed to the pope, and an embassy to Rome was prepared by Patriarch of Jerusalem Thomas, but it did not take place because of the political turmoil that swept Palestine after the death of Harun al-Rashid.[102]

The second wave of iconoclasm, which began in the Byzantine Empire in 814, provoked sharp condemnation from the Orthodox East. The leader of the Byzantine iconodules, Theodore the Studite was in correspondence with Patriarch Thomas of Jerusalem who, in turn, appealed to the emperor and patriarch in Constantinople to renounce the iconoclast heresy. In 814, representatives of Patriarch of Jerusalem Michael Syncellus and the monks Job, Theodore, and Theophanes went to Byzantium and denounced iconoclast doctrine, for which they underwent years of imprisonment and cruel punishment.[103]

After the final triumph of the veneration of icons in 842, Michael, Theodore, and Theophanes remained in Byzantium, adding to the number of Palestinian monks who settled in Constantinople. This colony of emigrants from the Holy Land, grouped around the Monastery of Chora, played a prominent role in the cultural exchange between Byzantium and the Middle East. In this milieu, supposedly, a number of literary monuments that were well known at that time were composed, such as the apocryphal epistle from the three Eastern patriarchs in defense of icons of 836 or the *Life of Theodore of Edessa* from the middle of the tenth century.[104]

Later, in cases of religious conflict in Constantinople, parties often deemed it necessary to appeal to the opinion of Alexandria, Antioch, and Jerusalem. Thus, members of the Middle Eastern Churches were involved in the debate over the case of Patriarch of Constantinople Photius in the 860s and 870s, but they did not stake out an independent position on the issue.

Persecution

Relations with Muslim authorities, the religious policy of the Caliphate, and the degree of Muslim tolerance for other faiths exerted a decisive influence on the development of the Middle Eastern Christian communities.

The first two centuries of the Muslim empire, especially the Umayyad era, were distinguished by a fairly high level of tolerance, in which Christians could worship freely, were active in commerce, and held prominent positions in the administration of the state. Harassment of Christians sometimes occurred in the provinces (e.g., Egyptian Coptic sources note five waves of persecution from the mid-680s to 717), which was more often motivated by the greed of governors than by religious intolerance.[105]

From what has been said regarding the religious policies of the Umayyads and the early ʿAbbasids, it is clear that real incidents of religious persecution in the eighth and beginning of the ninth centuries were isolated cases. The Christians' misfortunes, so colorfully described in some chronicles, especially those of the Syrian Jacobites, were rather caused by social oppression or civil instability. For example, in the story about the death of the twenty Sabaite Fathers killed in the Muslim civil wars in 796, the hagiographer pointedly and at length argued for the legitimacy of regarding the dead to be martyrs, even though they could not technically be considered to have suffered for their faith.[106]

In the second ʿAbbasid century, however, the nature of interfaith relations in the Caliphate began to change. In the mid-ninth century, the increasingly obvious crisis of the

Caliphate and the weakening of the Islamic world spawned a surge of fundamentalist sentiment among Muslims, which resulted in growing religious intolerance against *dhimmis*.

Periodic bans on the construction and expansion of churches started to be applied. Amid the unrest and anarchy after the death of Harun al-Rashid, Patriarch Thomas of Jerusalem undertook an unauthorized rebuilding of the dome of the Church of the Holy Sepulchre. After stable state power was restored, the patriarch was prosecuted for increasing the height of the dome and was able to exculpate himself only with great difficulty.[107]

The ʿAbbasid caliph al-Mutawakkil (847–861) waged a systematic persecution of infidels, desiring to strengthen in every way Sunni orthodoxy by suppressing unorthodox sects and movements in Islam as well as the non-Islamic communities. The caliph issued a series of decrees against non-Muslims, placing more stringent constraints and prohibitions on them. *Dhimmis* were ordered to wear special distinctive clothing and were forbidden to ride on horseback or to hold any position in the public service. All churches built after the Muslim conquest were subject to destruction. The abuses of the caliphal administration prompted a revolt by the people of Emesa (Homs) in 855. They were joined by the local Christians, who were pushed to take this step by religious persecution. After the uprising was suppressed, the caliph ordered all churches in the city destroyed and the Christian population driven out. Al-Mutawakkil's persecution led to a massive conversion of *dhimmis* to Islam and the emigration of a significant proportion of the Melkites to Byzantium.[108]

After al-Mutawakkil, Christians managed to recover in part their positions in the state administration, but this caused an ever-growing resentment from ordinary Muslims. At the end of the ninth century and especially in the first third of the tenth century, numerous cases of religious strife and unrest, looting, and the destruction of churches are mentioned. A particularly powerful wave of anti-Christian pogroms swept across the Middle East in the years 923–924, when the Melkite churches in Tinnis, Ashkalon, Ramla, Caesarea, and Damascus were destroyed. In 937, the churches of Jerusalem were attacked and in 940 the church in Ashkelon was once more destroyed and was never rebuilt.[109] These shocks provoked the appearance of one of the earliest original works of Christian Arabic literature, a lament over the sack of the Maryamiyya Cathedral of Damascus in 924. The anonymous author, apparently a member of the clergy of Damascus, attempted to support his coreligionists in a situation of intense psychological trauma and to convince them that the Melkites were still God's chosen people.[110]

The Byzantine Reconquista

By the 930s, the once mighty Caliphate had fallen into complete decline and broken up into a number of principalities. Egypt, Palestine, and southern Syria were successively ruled by the Turkic Tulunid (869–905) and Ikhshidid (935–969) dynasties. The greater part of northern Syria and Upper Mesopotamia was ruled by the Arab Hamdanid dynasty. Baghdad itself was captured by the Buyids in 945, and the caliphs only retained a shadow of spiritual power. At the same time, the Byzantine Empire launched an offensive against the weakened and feuding Muslim states. In 926, Malatya fell. In 942, the Byzantines, who were at the walls of Edessa, forced the Muslims to hand over to them the city's greatest relic, the image of Christ Not Made by Hands.[111] The greatest success of the Byzantine Reconquista was achieved in the 960s under the leadership of Nicephoras Phocas, who sought to give the Byzantine campaign the character of a holy war against Islam and—as the Arabs believed—saw his mission as being to liberate the Holy Sepulchre and to crush the Kaaba.[112] Nicephoras won a series of brilliant victories over the Muslims and returned Crete, Cyprus, Cilicia, and parts of northern Syria to the empire. The Hamdanids of Aleppo long acknowledged themselves to be vassals of the Byzantine Empire and paid a tribute from which, it was stipulated, local Christians were exempt.[113]

The Muslims' military failures and the influx of refugees from areas conquered by Byzantium greatly exacerbated sectarian tensions in the Middle East. Each triumph by Nicephoras Phocas provoked anti-Christian pogroms in Egypt, Palestine, and Syria. In 960 and 961, Muslim mobs burned and plundered the churches of Fustat, making no distinction between those of the Orthodox and the Monophysites.[114]

In 966, as a result of a conflict with the governor of Jerusalem, Patriarch John of Jerusalem was killed and the Church of the Holy Sepulchre was burned. In 967, Patriarch Christopher of Antioch was killed on charges of having ties with Byzantium. The true cause of his murder was a long-standing dispute between certain Muslim sheikhs and the patriarch, who was more loyal to the Hamdanid emir Sayf al-Dawla than to the regional elite of Antioch. However, in an atmosphere of interreligious conflict when five thousand horsemen from Khorasan arrived to take part in jihad, it was very easy to declare the patriarch a Byzantine spy and, after his murder, to organize the looting of the patriarchal residence and the Church of St Cassian. After that, the See of Antioch was vacant until the Byzantines captured the city in the autumn of 969.[115]

Muslim attempts to recapture the city in 971 and 994 were unsuccessful. The new Byzantine emperor John Tzimiskes devastated Upper Mesopotamia in 972 and then, seeing a serious rival in the Egyptian Fatimids, marched into southern Syria and Palestine in 974 and 975, briefly seizing Damascus and almost reaching Jerusalem. The emperor's sudden death halted Byzantine expansion for a time. After the military campaigns of Basil II the Bulgar-Slayer in Syria in 995 and 999, the political situation on the Byzantine–Muslim frontier stabilized for half a century. There was a bipolar system in the Middle East based on the balance between two great powers: the Byzantine Empire, which controlled a large part of northern Syria, and the Fatimid Caliphate, whose border ran through Lebanon and southern Syria. The two empires had a buffer zone centered in Aleppo, which was first a vassal of the Byzantine Empire and then, in 1015, was captured by the Fatimids. The final success of the Byzantine Reconquista was the capture of Edessa in 1031, resulting in nearly half the Patriarchate of Antioch finding itself once again in the Christian empire.[116]

The empire's military expansion was paralleled by the strengthening of Byzantine cultural influence in the Middle East. In 937, the patriarch of Constantinople asked his three Eastern brethren to commemorate him in the liturgy, something that had not been done since the days of the Umayyads.[117] In the middle of the tenth century, a revision of the Typicon of the Church of Jerusalem was undertaken, incorporating liturgical texts of Constantinopolitan origin. In the main churches of Jerusalem, the services themselves were apparently celebrated in Greek.[118]

Christians and the Fatimids

As the Byzantine Empire extended its rule over northern Syria, the territories of the patriarchates of Alexandria and Jerusalem and the remaining portion of the Patriarchate of Antioch found itself within the Shiite Fatimid Caliphate, which opposed the ʿAbbasids of Baghdad.

The Fatimid Caliphate represented a typical universal state with claims to possess absolute truth and the desire for world domination. The chief ambition of the Fatimid caliphs was the overthrow of the ʿAbbasids of Baghdad, but they were able to extend their authority no further than southern Syria and western Arabia. The Ismaili empire with its center in Cairo was surrounded by a belt of vassal territories, among which the Fatimids also counted the Christian countries of northeast Africa—Nubia and Ethiopia. The See of the apostle Mark in Alexandria remained the spiritual center for the Christians of the entire Nile Valley and the Fatimids invariably used the authority of the Coptic patriarch to build relations with their Christian neighbors to the south.[119]

The imperial character of the Fatimid state, as well as the fact that Ismailis remained a minority in Egypt, meant that there was a high degree of religious tolerance on the part of the caliphs, including toward Christians. The Fatimid era is considered the high point of the development of Egyptian Christianity under Islam.

The dynasty required educated administrators. The Fatimids made use of the Ikhshidid bureaucracy that they had inherited, in which Christians were predominant. Under the early caliphs—al-Muʿizz (952–975), al-ʿAziz (975–996), and the early reign of al-Hakim (996–1021)—*dhimmis* held the highest government positions, including the post of vizier, something that had no analogue in either the Muslim world or earlier Egyptian history.

Under al-Muʿizz and al-ʿAziz, a key role in the administration of Egypt was played by Yaʿqub ibn Killis (d. 991), a convert to Islam from an Iraqi Jewish background. His chief rival in the 970s was the Coptic official Quzman ibn Mina, who had served under the Ikhshidids and under the Fatimids headed the tax authority in Palestine and held other prominent positions in the financial administration. In 993, the Christian ʿIsa ibn Nasturas rose to the position of vizier. After the death of al-ʿAziz, ʿIsa was accused of financial malfeasance as a result of court intrigues and was killed in early 997. In the following years, until the caliph al-Hakim came of age, affairs of state were governed by the eunuch Barjuwan, whose right hand man was the Christian secretary Fahd ibn Ibrahim. In the year 1000, al-Hakim had his regent executed and placed Fahd in the post of vizier.

The dominance of "infidels" at the court provoked a backlash among Muslims and attacks on the caliphs themselves, but an effective apparatus of repression allowed the Fatimids to extinguish any discontent.[120]

Thus, for example, in 993, when the navy that had been constructed for a campaign against Byzantium burned down in Cairo's naval shipyards, the Cairo mob accused the "infidels" of starting the fire and launched a pogrom against Christians. Dozens of rioters were arrested on the spot and some of them, chosen by lot, were executed. The authorities also announced that anyone appropriating goods stolen from the Christians during the riots would also be punished with death, and so during the night, thieves discarded their loot in the desert.[121]

During the Fatimids' first decades, there are many cases of churches being restored and even the construction of new Christian places of worship, despite the protests of some fanatically minded Muslims. By the tenth century, Muslim jurists and the general public had become entrenched in the opinion that the construction of new places of worship by *dhimmis* was illegal. The Fatimid caliphs, however, considered themselves to be the bearers of divine grace and the source of law, so they did not need approval for their actions from religious authorities. Several churches appeared in the Fatimid capital of al-Qahira (Cairo), which retained the character of a closed city for the elite.

The Fatimid caliphs, like their Ikhshidid predecessors, visited monasteries and attended Christian religious festivals such as Theophany and Palm Sunday. The broad participation of Muslims in these celebrations bears witness to the syncretistic character of Medieval Egyptian culture and confirms the blending of the identities of the Christian and Muslim populations. There was a tradition of distributing money to courtiers on Muslim holidays and similar distributions took place on Holy Thursday and Coptic New Year (Nayrouz) as well.[122]

The caliph al-ʿAziz was married to an Orthodox Egyptian and strongly patronized the Melkite community. He furnished his brothers-in-law with distinguished ecclesiastical careers—Orestes was enthroned patriarch of Jerusalem and Arsenius became metropolitan of Cairo in 985. Orestes completed the restoration of the Church of the Holy Sepulchre in Jerusalem, which, as mentioned earlier, had been attacked in 966. Arsenius, with the support of the Muslim authorities, seized churches from the Copts that previously had belonged to the Orthodox.

At the end of the tenth century, the Melkites clearly occupied the leading position among all the non-Muslim confessions of the Fatimid state. Orestes, an Orthodox monk and the caliph's son-in-law, was ideally suited for diplomatic missions connected to Fatimid–Byzantine relations. In the early 980s he was sent to Sicily to resolve a conflict between the Byzantines and the emir of Sicily, a Fatimid vassal. In 1000, Orestes, who was already patriarch of Jerusalem, went as the head of an embassy to Constantinople for peace negotiations. At the same time, according to a Christian chronicle, the vizier Barjuwan promised in advance on behalf of the young caliph al-Hakim to accept any peace conditions that the patriarch could manage to negotiate. Orestes remained in Constantinople until his death in 1005. The Patriarchate of Jerusalem de facto came under the leadership of his brother Arsenius, who in 1000 had been installed by orders of the caliph on the patriarchal throne of Alexandria. Thus, Arsenius, the maternal uncle of the ruling caliph, concentrated leadership in his hands over the entire Orthodox community in the Fatimid Caliphate.[123]

The prosperity of the Melkites and other *dhimmis* under the early Fatimids, however, ended abruptly at the beginning of the eleventh century, when the Muslims' accumulated discontent boiled over. This period is closely tied to the personality of the caliph al-Hakim, who launched the most severe persecution of *dhimmis* starting in 1003. The harshness of the caliph's anti-Christian decrees was exacerbated by his mental illness, paranoia, and ruthlessness; al-Hakim seriously sought to eradicate people of other religions, who made up almost half of his subjects.

Each successive year was marked by massive pogroms against churches and Christian quarters and the desecration of Christian cemeteries. With few exceptions, all monasteries and thousands of churches in the Fatimid realm were destroyed, and mosques often were erected over their sites. Crosses were removed from the surviving churches and images of crosses were scratched from their walls. In 1008, the caliph forbade Christians from celebrating the Entry of the Lord into Jerusalem, then Epiphany. There were periodic purges of the state administration, accompanied by the arrest, torture, and execution of Christian officials. In their place, however, other Christians were hired, so Egypt was lacking in qualified Muslim bureaucrats. Starting in 1005, a variety of restrictions were placed on the clothing of *dhimmis*. Christians were ordered to dress in black and wear heavy wooden crosses around their necks, the size of which increased with each subsequent decree.[124]

Al-Hakim's anti-Christian policies reached their apogee in 1009 with the destruction of the Christians' most revered shrine, the Holy Sepulchre, as well as several other Palestinian churches and monasteries. Soon thereafter in 1010, the Egyptian Melkites' main monastery, al-Qusayr on Mount Muqattam near Cairo, was laid waste and the adjacent cemetery was desecrated and destroyed. Patriarch Arsenius ever more clearly understood that his kinship with the half-mad caliph did not guarantee his safety. Tormented by dark forebodings, he spent his time in prayer and fasting, something to which he does not seem to have been inclined during the early, brilliant part of his career. Arsenius could not evade death: in the summer of that year, he was secretly killed on the caliph's orders.[125]

Toward the end of 1010, Palestine and Syria were captured by the Bedouin leader Mufarrij ibn al-Jarrah, who successfully resisted the Fatimids for almost three years. Wishing to keep his borders with Byzantium secure, Mufarrij made a point of favoring the Christians: thus, he organized the elections of the new patriarch of Jerusalem, Theophilus (1012–1020), who was a bishop in Transjordan, and supported the beginning of the rebuilding of the Holy Sepulchre. After Mufarrij's death and the restoration of

Fatimid power in Syria, Patriarch Theophilus fled, but then returned at the invitation of the authorities.[126]

At the same time in Egypt, the activities of the Orthodox Church were paralyzed. Empty sees were not replaced and only one Melkite bishop survived the era of al-Hakim. In 1014, the caliph allowed *dhimmis* to migrate out of Egypt and a mass exodus of Christians to Byzantine territory began. Of the remaining non-Muslims in Egypt, a significant proportion accepted Islam, often disingenuously. In the final years of his reign, al-Hakim was fascinated by a new religious quest and halted the persecution of Christians, even turning a blind eye to violations of his own anti-Christian decrees.[127]

The next caliph, al-Zahir (1021–1035), and the regent Sitt al-Mulk, al-Hakim's sister, canceled all the restrictions imposed on non-Muslims. The Orthodox were able to elect a new patriarch and bishops. Christians who had fled Egypt returned and restored their ruined churches. Church holidays were once more observed in all their splendor, and even those who had been forcibly converted to Islam converted back to Christianity without punishment.

Subsequent Fatimid caliphs likewise tolerated Christians and allowed them to hold key government positions.[128] This, however, did not prevent Muslim officials from occasionally solving their own financial problems at the expense of the Christian community. Under pressure from Muslim public opinion, the caliphs sometimes fired Christian officials and levied heavy taxes on the *dhimmis*.

The patriarchs of Jerusalem once more acted as intermediaries in the reestablishment of relations between

Byzantium and the Fatimids. In 1023, Patriarch Nicephorus was sent by Sitt al-Mulk to Constantinople with a message about the restoration of the rights of Christians in Egypt and a request for the resumption of trade and the conclusion of a peace treaty. Negotiations continued in 1032. Emperor Romanus III sought for himself the privilege to appoint the patriarch of Jerusalem and to rebuild the Church of the Holy Sepulchre. The final agreement was signed in 1036/1037. Byzantium got the opportunity to rebuild the church in all its glory, which was accomplished in the 1040s. The grandiose building made a strong impression on contemporaries.[129]

A new increase in the Georgian presence in Palestine dates to this same period, made visibly manifest in the construction of the Georgian Monastery of the Holy Cross a few kilometers to the south of Jerusalem in the second quarter of the eleventh century.

Byzantine Antioch

In the late tenth and eleventh centuries the historical destiny of the Melkites of the Byzantine part of Syria (the provinces of Antioch, Cilicia, Malatya, and others) evolved under different circumstances. A significant proportion of the population of these territories was made up of Arabic-speaking Christians, both Orthodox and Jacobite, as well as Muslims.

During the reign of the emperor Romanus (1028–1034), Byzantine authorities began to persecute the Jacobites. Their patriarch and some bishops were exiled to Thrace, other bishops accepted Orthodoxy, and the rest died in exile. After that, the Syriac Jacobites moved their patriarchal throne to Muslim territory, to Amida (Diyabakir).

Characteristically, after the Byzantines captured Edessa in 1031, the local Jacobite Christians left the city for Muslim territory, although a significant proportion of them later returned. The persecution of heretics in the Byzantine border regions was periodically renewed. In the 1060s, the

Jacobite bishop of Malatya was sent to Macedonia, where for three years he worked in the fields and vineyards.[130] Monophysite chronicles recount that the Lord was angry with the Chalcedonians for their persecution of the true Christian believers and incinerated by lightening all the Greek churches of Antioch and killed the Byzantine patriarch of Antioch, who, during an earthquake, was swallowed up by the earth with ten thousand of his coreligionists.[131] The origin of this legend is perhaps due to the catastrophic earthquake that destroyed many cities of Western Asia in 1053.

The governors of Antioch were as a rule Greeks coming from the military nobility or state officials. Representatives of the Arab Christian aristocracy also played an important role in the life of the province, such as the magister 'Ubaydallah or the patrician Kulayb, who participated in the confrontation between the rebel Bardas Skleros and the emperor Basil II in the 970s.[132]

At times, the patriarch of Antioch had great political clout. Among the primates of the Church of Antioch in the late tenth and eleventh centuries are found natives of the central regions of the Byzantine Empire (Greeks and Armenian Chalcedonians) and, during the first decades of Byzantine power, Syro-Palestinian Arabs. A major figure in this series is Patriarch Agapius (978–996), previously metropolitan of Aleppo. After the death of Patriarch Theodore of Antioch (970–976), Agapius took a list of potential candidates to fill the vacant throne to Constantinople for confirmation by Emperor Basil II. At this time, amid the rebellion of Bardas Skleros, Antioch fell away from the emperor's authority and joined the rebels. Agapius told Basil II, whose military situation at the time was difficult, that he would return Antioch to Constantinople's rule, asking as a reward to be elevated to the patriarchal see of Antioch. Both strong personalities, the emperor and the metropolitan understood that it was expedient for them to become allies. Returning to Syria in secret, Agapius came into contact with the magister 'Ubaydallah, the governor of Antioch, on the emperor's behalf and convinced the governor to go over to the side of Basil II. Bardas Skleros tried to regain the city several times but failed. In 977, the emperor suppressed the rebellion, and Skleros fled to Muslim territory. For services rendered to the empire, on January 22, 978, Agapius was elevated to the rank of patriarch of Antioch. In later years, he played a key role in the regional elite of Antioch. The patriarch became friends with the Domestic of the Scholae of the East,[133] Bardas Phocas, and tacitly supported his ambitious plan to seize the imperial throne. As a result, in 987, Phocas's revolt began, with Agapius and the provincial elite standing behind him. Apparently, they hoped to increase his role in the administration of the empire. After the defeat and death of Bardas Phocas in the spring of 989, Agapius, attempting to exonerate himself before Basil II, led a rebellion of the people of Antioch against Phocas's governor, his son Leo. Bardas's secret correspondence fell into the emperor's hands, however, and the patriarch's involvement in the rebellion was revealed. In late 989, he was exiled from his see to Constantinople. Oddly enough, Basil II, famous for his ruthlessness, for some reason did not touch Agapius. The latter spent seven years in the capital under virtual house arrest, while continuing to manage the affairs of his patriarchate. In September 996, after the emperor's persistent coaxing, Agapius agreed to abdicate in exchange for a lifetime pension and the retention of his name in the diptychs. He died a year later in one of the monasteries of Constantinople.[134] According to Nikon of the Black Mountain, a Byzantine canonist of the eleventh century, from this time the custom was established of consecrating the patriarch of Antioch in the empire's capital.[135]

The emperors participated in the election of the patriarchs of Antioch, wanting to see them as reliable servants of the empire. Nevertheless, the patriarchs often behaved quite independently toward Constantinople. The most famous example of this is associated with the figure of Patriarch Peter III of Antioch (1050s), who jealously guarded the independence of his see against the claims of the patriarch of Constantinople. In particular, Peter took a special, mediating stance in the conflict between Rome and Constantinople in 1054, which led to the final break between Orthodoxy and Catholicism. Antioch's position was determined in particular by disagreement over the See of Constantinople's policy of unifying church rituals. This was unacceptable to the ethnically diverse Patriarchate of Antioch, where the liturgy continued to be celebrated alongside Greek in Syriac and Arabic.[136]

The formation of the Orthodox Arabs' cultural foundation, which had begun with Theodore Abu Qurra and his contemporaries, occurred in a very short time. With northern Syria returned to the bosom of the empire, Byzantium found

that there was an already well-established Arabic-speaking
Christian ethnic group there. During four generations of
Byzantine rule, it did not show even the slightest inclina-
tion to assimilate. The Antioch of the late tenth and eleventh
centuries was a major center of Christian culture, both in
Greek and in Arabic. Halfway between the city and the sea,
on the spur of the rock massif of the Black Mountain, there
flourished a constellation of monasteries where monks of
Greek, Georgian, Arabic, and Armenian origin labored and
an active literary life unfolded. The most notable Byzantine
writer from this milieu was Nikon of the Black Mountain,
the leading expert in the field of canon law in the second
half of the eleventh century. Some of the patriarchs of Antioch, such as Theodore III and Peter III, were also known
for their theological works. The aforementioned Patriarch
Agapius in the late tenth century was also a gifted writer.
The Orthodox Arabs' center of cultural creativity moved
from Southern Palestine to Antioch. The historian Yahya
of Antioch (d. after 1034), a native of Egypt who moved
to Antioch in 1015, continued the chronicle of Eutychius
(Sa'id ibn Batriq).[137] The great luminary of medical science
of that age, the Baghdad native Ibn Butlan, who authored
many treatises of a theoretical and practical character and
works on geography, ethnography, and anthropology, was
active in Antioch in the 1060s.[138] An Arabic-language hagiographic literature developed. In the late tenth century, the
protospatharios[139] Ibrahim ibn Yuhanna wrote the Life of
Patriarch Christopher who, as mentioned earlier, died at the
hands of Muslims shortly before the Byzantines reconquered

Antioch.[140] In 1085, the hieromonk Michael wrote the first biography of St John of Damascus, which was immediately translated into several languages.[141] An important milestone in the development of Arabic Christian theology was the work of the deacon 'Abdallah ibn al-Fadl (d. c. 1051). In addition to compiling his own interpretations and teachings on the Holy Scriptures, 'Abdallah collected all the versions of the Arabic Bible that were in use, compared them with the Greek original, edited them, and put into use a complete Arabic version of the Old and New Testament that was used in the Orthodox Church for many centuries.[142]

Although Melkite culture began once more to experience a strong Greek influence starting in the middle of the tenth century, it did not dissolve into a common imperial Greek–Byzantine culture, but rather it maintained its oriental identity and remained in close contact with the rest of the Arab world.

The authority of the patriarch of Antioch extended to the most remote parts of the Muslim world—Marv[143] and Khwarezm.[144] The border between Byzantium and the Muslim states was not an obstacle for lively cultural inter-actions. The influence of the Arab tradition is so marked that in his chronicle, Yahya of Antioch uses AH dating[145] (as does Eutychius) and both Yahya and Patriarch Agapius begin their works with the phrase "bismillah al-rahman al-rahim" (in the name of God, the munificent, the merciful) instead of the traditional Christian formula "in the name of the Father, Son, and Holy Spirit." Yahya is much more interested in the political history of Egypt and Syria than the wars of his own emperor, Basil the Bulgar-Slayer in the Balkans.[146] The most striking example, however, is the debate among Christians of different countries and denominations over the date of Easter in 1007. On account of differences in calculations and tables, there was vigorous correspondence, consultation, wrangling, and debate in which participated Melkites, Nestorians, and Monophysites from Armenia to Upper Egypt.[147] It is curious that Constantinople remained on the periphery of this dispute, as though the Ecumenical Patriarch meant little to Middle Eastern Christians, even to the Melkites of Byzantine Antioch. Even less did they think of Rome. Even though, according to custom, the pope's name was proclaimed during the liturgy, because of a lack of connections with Rome, no one knew these names. The last pope known to the East, as mentioned earlier, was Agapius, who participated in the Sixth Ecumenical Council in 681. He was commemorated, as a formality, for the next three hundred years.[148]

The relative political stability that was established in Syria was destroyed in the middle of the eleventh century by the arrival of the Seljuk Turks and their devastating raids on the towns of Upper Mesopotamia. The Byzantine Empire's decisive clash with the Seljuks at Manzikert in 1071 ended with the complete defeat of the Byzantines and the empire's losing control of almost the whole of Asia Minor.

The situation was aggravated by internal unrest in the Byzantine Empire and the struggle for the throne among various claimants. Antioch was also actively involved in these riots and civil wars of the 1070s. Patriarch Emilian played an active role in the city's affairs and was hostile to the government of Emperor Michael VII Doukas. In 1073, the new governor of Antioch sent from the capital, Isaac Comnenus, managed by cunning to lure the patriarch out of the city and send him to Constantinople and to suppress the brewing revolt of the people of Antioch.[149] Nevertheless, some time later, northern Syria was lost to the empire.

In the atmosphere of political chaos afflicting Asia Minor after the catastrophe of Manzikert, an Orthodox Armenian, the former Byzantine dignitary Philaretos Brachamios (Varajnuni), managed to create an autonomous principality out of the wreckage of Byzantine provinces including Cilicia, Antioch, Malatya, and Edessa, but it had no real power to resist the Muslim onslaught. In 1084, the sultan of Iconium, Sulayman ibn Kutlumush, invaded the Christian territories of northern Syria without encountering any serious resistance. In December 1084, the Seljuks seized Antioch with a surprise attack. The city returned to Muslim rule and the Cathedral of St Cassian was converted into a mosque.[150]

However, the Turkish emir Yaghi-Siyan, who became ruler of Antioch around 1087, allowed the Orthodox patriarch to return to the city. This patriarch was John the Oxite, who came from the Greek clergy, and was a prominent church writer and an uncompromising lover of truth with a difficult personality. Already as a monk he wrote a treatise against the charisticariate, the practice of members of the Byzantine aristocracy establishing their own monasteries, which, according to John, led to the degradation of the institution of monasticism. In the early 1090s, the patriarch sent

the emperor Alexius Comnenus two angry letters in which
he sharply criticized his policies, particularly the confiscation of church property, and held the emperor responsible
for the state's domestic and foreign problems. In his pam-
phlets, John also condemned the Byzantine aristocracy and
bureaucracy that brutally oppressed the poor. In Antioch,
the patriarch polemicized against the Syrian Monotheletes. A treatise on the two wills of Christ was written by
the Maronite bishop Tuma of al-Kfartab in response to the
Oxite's attacks.[151]

In itself, the establishment of Seljuk rule in the Middle
East in the late eleventh century did not result in a noticeable deterioration of the social status of local Christians.[152]
In the eleventh century, the Muslim jurist al-Mawardi
formulated another, rather clearly set forth doctrine on the
status of *dhimmis* in a Muslim state that would have a great
influence on the legal practice of subsequent generations of
rulers. Protection was to be granted to non-Muslim subjects
when they met six mandatory and six desirable conditions.
The first group of conditions included not denouncing the
Qur'an, the prophet Muhammad, or the religion of Islam;
not marrying a Muslim woman; not inducing a Muslim to
renounce his faith; and not aiding enemies of Islam. Failure
to comply with any of these conditions placed the infidel
outside the law. Desirable conditions included the wearing
of distinctive clothing, the prohibition against constructing
buildings taller than those of the Muslims, ringing bells,
displaying crosses, publicly drinking wine, holding noisy
funeral processions, and riding horses. Violation of these

statutes did not involve the loss of "protected" status but was nevertheless punished. The everyday restrictions ("desirable conditions," according to Mawardi), however, were little respected in real life, although from time to time pious rulers attempted to revive them.

For the most part, Christians of that era, like the rest of the population, suffered from the political instability in Syria, the endless wars between miniature emirates, and the violent repartition of territory. Thus, as a result of civil wars between Seljuk rulers and general instability in Palestine, Patriarch Symeon of Jerusalem with his bishops left the Holy Land and moved to Cyprus in the second half of the 1090s (the exact date is unknown). Archbishop John of Tyre, who shortly before had fled to Palestine from Tyre to escape persecution from the Fatimid vizier, came to be the leader of the Palestinian clergy.[153]

The First Crusade

The balance of power in the Eastern Mediterranean changed dramatically in 1097 with the arrival of the European Crusaders who came to liberate the Holy Land from the Muslim yoke. Crossing into Asia, the Crusaders cut through the domain of the Seljuk Sultanate of Iconium and arrived at Antioch. As the bulk of the Crusader army was besieging the city, in the spring of 1098, one of the leaders of the campaign, Baldwin of Flanders, took control of Edessa, where he established a Christian state. A significant proportion of the local Christians, especially the Armenians of Cilicia and the region of the Euphrates, willingly supported the Crusaders. The Orthodox and Syrian Jacobites behaved rather passively. Nevertheless, with the appearance of the Western knights under the walls of Antioch, the ruler of the city, Yaghi-Siyan (a vassal of the Seljuks of Aleppo), found it necessary to take repressive measures against the local Christians. Patriarch John the Oxite was imprisoned, non-Muslims were persecuted, and the Cathedral of St Peter was turned into stables. According to chroniclers, during the siege of Antioch, the Turks hung the patriarch in a cage on the city wall before the eyes of the Crusaders as a way of vilifying the Christian faith. After a seven-month siege, on June 2, 1098, the Crusaders captured Antioch. The Muslim garrison was slaughtered and the city plundered.

The following year, the army of European knights marched into Palestine. With the Crusaders approaching in June 1099, Muslim residents fled Ramla, after destroying the enormous Church of St George that stood among the ruins of neighboring Lydda. Residents of the Christian city of Bethlehem went out to meet the procession of the "Frankish" army, welcoming their liberators. The Muslim governor of Jerusalem (which the Fatimids had managed to regain shortly before) ordered Christians to leave the city to save food in case of a siege. The Crusaders took Jerusalem on July 14, 1099. During the assault, the city's entire remaining population, Muslim and Jewish, was slaughtered.

On the territories conquered from the Muslims, there appeared Christian states: the Kingdom of Jerusalem, the County of Tripoli, the Principality of Antioch, and the County of Edessa.[154]

With the victory of the Franks (Europeans), the situation of Syrian Christians did not improve. The Latins prevented their Eastern coreligionists from having full social standing. There could be no question of admitting them to the ranks of the ruling class. The lands of the Crusader states were divided between European barons, the military orders, and hierarchs of the Latin Church. The local population soon felt the brunt of the Western feudal system and the level of exploitation became higher than it had been previously. Among other things, the Crusaders sought to subjugate Middle Eastern Christians—"schismatics" and "heretics"— to the authority of the Papal See.

Historians identify different trends in the Crusaders' religious policy. Accompanying the First Crusade was the papal legate, Bishop Adhemar of Le Puy, who tried to maintain friendly relations with the Eastern Christians and cooperated with the patriarch of Jerusalem, Symeon, who was then in Cyprus. Adhemar, however, died during the epidemic that followed the capture of Antioch, where they left a mountain of corpses to rot. With his death, the intolerance of the Franks burst out into the open.[155]

The Banishment of the Patriarchs

Immediately upon taking the Holy City, the Crusaders organized an election for the Latin patriarch of Jerusalem. This was followed by the displacement of the hierarchy of the Orthodox Church in the Holy Land and its replacement with Latin clergy, to whom the Eastern Christians were subject. Sites of veneration and the best churches were transferred to the Catholics, who also appropriated the most valuable relics, including particles of the Precious Cross, which were forcibly seized from the Orthodox.[156] Like the previous Muslim rulers of the Holy Land, the Crusaders allowed other religious communities—Muslims, Jews, Samaritans, and Christians of the non-Chalcedonian churches—to have internal autonomy. At the same time, the Franks did yet not consider the Melkites to be "heterodox" and therefore tried to integrate them into the Catholic Church.

According to later Western chroniclers, the Orthodox patriarch of Jerusalem Symeon died in the summer of 1099, almost simultaneously with the capture of Jerusalem by the Crusaders.[157] Thus, the Franks had the formal right to fill the vacant patriarchal see. In Orthodox historiography, however, it is widely believed that Patriarch Symeon was still alive in 1106 (his own anti-Latin treatise on azymes references a document dated to 1105).[158] Thus, the election of the Latin patriarch of Jerusalem occurred while there was a living Orthodox primate.

After the death of Symeon, John VIII, formerly the archbishop of Tyre, was chosen as the new Orthodox patriarch. According to some reports, the election was held in Jerusalem; it is unclear what was the attitude of the Latin authorities toward this and what status John had in their eyes.[159] In any case, he already moved to Byzantium by 1107/1108, where he remained until his death. A succession of the Orthodox patriarchs of Jerusalem in exile was formed in Constantinople. The Byzantine emperors attached a great deal of importance to preserving the succession of the Orthodox patriarchs of the Holy Land as a symbol of their claim to be the protectors of Palestinian Orthodoxy. The patriarchs had their residence at the Monastery of St Diomides in Constantinople. Among them were major theologians and church leaders who played a prominent role in Byzantine history in the twelfth century.[160]

Only one of the primates of Jerusalem of this era tried to exercise his pastoral ministry in Palestine. Patriarch Leontius (1176–1185) arrived in the Holy Land but was not allowed by the Latin authorities to serve in the Church of the Holy Sepulchre, which he could visit only as a simple pilgrim. The patriarch settled in Bethlehem, where several attempts were made on his life. The emir of Damascus invited Leontius to move to his territory, but the patriarch declined the invitation. Only at the insistence of Emperor Manuel Comnenus and out of a desire not to provoke sectarian violence in Palestine did Leontius return to Constantinople.[161]

Many Orthodox bishops of the Patriarchate of Jerusalem were forced to leave their sees upon the arrival of the Crusaders. It is known that Savvas, metropolitan of Caesarea, which was captured in 1101 by King Baldwin of Jerusalem, left for the territory of the Fatimids and later is presumed to have become patriarch of Alexandria. The sources also mention a metropolitan of Tiberias who lived in exile in Constantinople in the 1120s.[162]

Relations between the Orthodox and the Latins in the Patriarchate of Antioch were even more dramatic. The Crusaders initially treated John the Oxite, the patriarch of Antioch, with a great deal of reverence. The papal legate Adhemar of Le Puy confirmed him in the dignity of patriarch as head of both the Orthodox and the Latin clergy of Antioch.[163] Soon, however (following Steven Runciman's modern-day interpretation), John's situation became complicated, as a result of Adhemar's message to the pope written in the summer of 1098 on behalf of Patriarch Symeon of Jerusalem. In this letter, Symeon was positioned as primate of all the Christians in the Middle East, without any mention of the patriarch of Antioch and his rights. On September 11, the leaders of the Crusader army sent a letter inviting the pope to come to the East and take the See of Antioch as the second see of the apostle Peter, alongside Rome. Such an invitation, as unrealistic as it was, demonstrates the Crusaders' disdain for the Orthodox patriarch of Antioch.[164]

In October 1098, the Crusaders captured the Muslim city of al-Bara near Apamea. John consecrated a Latin bishop for the city. Although there had not previously been an Orthodox hierarchy in the city, this act was the first step toward the creation of a parallel Latin church structure in the Middle East. After much debate among the leaders of the Crusade over the future of the city of Antioch, the city was retained by Prince Bohemond of Taranto. Many historians consider him to be the central figure in bringing about conflict between Byzantium and the Crusaders, a person who contributed to the irreversibility of the deepening schism between Rome and Constantinople.[165] Of all the Crusaders, he was the most hostile to Byzantium and the Orthodox patriarch of Antioch, whom he considered to be an agent of influence of the Byzantine Empire.

The prince of Antioch maintained close ties with the new papal legate, Dagobert, who became the Latin patriarch of Jerusalem in late 1099. Now Bohemond could completely ignore John. In violation of his rights, Dagobert personally installed Latin bishops in the Antiochian dioceses of Tarsus, Arta, Mamistra, and Edessa. The Crusaders suspected John of plotting to hand Antioch over to the Byzantine emperor. As a result of pressure from them, the patriarch was forced to leave the city sometime before August 1100. In his place, Bohemond installed the bishop of Arta, Bernard of Valence, from whom originated the line of Latin patriarchs of Antioch, subordinate to the pope.[166]

John the Oxite and the Orthodox bishops withdrew to Byzantium. There the elderly John resigned his patriarchal rank and his bishops elected a new patriarch. In this way, in parallel with the Latin patriarchs of Antioch, there continued a succession of Orthodox patriarchs in exile. Almost all of them came from the Greek clergy. Some of them played a prominent role in the life of the Byzantine Church, such as Athanasius I (1157–1171), who took part in theological disputes during the time of Manuel Comnenus, and Theodore Balsamon (1185–1203), the leading canonist in the Orthodox world at the turn of the twelfth to the thirteen century.

The Kingdom of Jerusalem

Despite the best efforts of the Crusaders to get rid of the Orthodox hierarchy, individual Orthodox bishops remained in Palestine. In pilgrimage literature and various documents of the twelfth century, there appear the Melkite bishop Samuel, who was in Jerusalem in the 1130s; Meletius, archbishop of the Greeks and Syrians of Gaza and Eleutheropolis (1173); and unnamed bishops of Lydda, Acre (Akka), and Scythopolis.[167] It is believed that these bishops performed auxiliary functions under the Latin bishops of Palestine, performing the services in the Byzantine rite and ordaining priests for the local Arab Christian population but without having any administrative authority.[168]

Against the background of the destruction of the ecclesiastical structures of the Patriarchate of Jerusalem, the flowering of the Palestinian monasteries stands in sharp contrast. By the time of the Crusaders' arrival in the Holy Land, a number of monasteries still existed. In the literature, there are claims that by the end of the eleventh century only two monasteries remained outside the walls of Jerusalem, Mar Saba and Holy Cross.[169] This, however, contradicts the testimony of a Russian pilgrim from 1106 to 1107, the abbot Daniel, about the monasteries of St Theodosius and St Chariton in the Judean wilderness remaining intact and the monasteries of St John Chrysostom and Kalamon in the Jordan Valley even prospering. Various sources also confirm the presence of three monasteries on Mount Tabor (later authors speak of two monasteries).[170]

The kings of Jerusalem tolerated the Orthodox monasteries and even provided them with protection. In the absence of an Orthodox patriarch in Palestine, the abbot of Mar Saba served as primate of the Orthodox population and clergy, as is evident from Daniel's description of the Easter celebrations in Jerusalem in 1107.[171] The favorable position of the Orthodox monasteries is explained by a certain contradiction in the interests of the papal curia and the kings of Jerusalem regarding maintaining friendly relations with Byzantium and the conclusion of dynastic marriages with Orthodox aristocratic families. The emperor Manuel Comnenus (1143–1180) sought to be the patron of universal Orthodoxy and took the opportunity to invest heavily in the restoration and decoration of Palestinian churches and monasteries. Moreover, competition did not arise between Latin and Orthodox monasteries for purely geographic reasons. The Catholic monasteries were established either in the vicinity of Jerusalem or in Galilee, in densely populated rural areas, whereas the Orthodox monasteries were located in the Judean Desert.[172]

According to several sources, primarily the Byzantine pilgrim John Phocas, a number of monasteries in the Holy Land were restored in the 1180s: in addition to those monasteries mentioned previously, the Monastery of the Prophet Elias between Jerusalem and Bethlehem, the Lavra of St Euthymius in the Judean hills, the Monastery of Koziba (Wadi Qelt), and the Monasteries of St Gerasimus and John the Baptist by the Jordan. The Monastery of the Prophet Elias on Mount Tabor was also renovated, with the nearby Monastery of the Transfiguration having passed into the hands of the Catholics. In the late twelfth century, Orthodox monks from Calabria revived the Monastery of the Prophet Elias on Mount Carmel over Haifa, but later Latin monks settled in the monastery (they had probably lived there for some time together with the Orthodox monks under the same rule), and it went into the jurisdiction of the Latin patriarch of Jerusalem.[173] Archaeological surveys have confirmed the renovation of the Monasteries of Koziba and St Gerasimus (Dayr Hajla), which also were decorated with new paintings. In the Monastery of St Gerasimus are preserved Greek inscriptions about the restoration of the monastery during the patriarchate of John (presumably John IX) under the abbot Jacob. Arabic inscriptions from Dayr Hajla and Wadi Qelt contain the names of the artisans who rebuilt the monasteries.[174]

In the Palestinian monasteries, monks gathered from around the Orthodox world. Most visible in the monastic community was the Greek element. At the same time, there was an increased presence of Georgian monks. There is evidence for the establishment of a Georgian women's monastery in Palestine in the 1120s.[175] Natives of the Slavic lands lived in the Palestinian monasteries, as evidenced, for example, by the Life of Euphrosyne of Polotsk. Notable is the presence of a community of Frankish monks even in Mar Saba, constituting one of the several autonomous ethnic groups living in the monastery. Historians have noticed traces of influence from the Byzantine monastic tradition on Catholic monasticism in the Kingdom of Jerusalem.[176]

The monasteries received generous contributions from Byzantium, Georgia, and other countries. These funds allowed the monasteries to acquire significant landholdings in various areas of Palestine, especially the Jordan Valley. There are documents conferring villages to Mar Saba by Queen Melisende of Jerusalem (1131–1162) as well as various land transactions of the Palestinian monasteries. According to John Phocas, the Jordan Valley was covered with gardens belonging to the monasteries of the Judean Desert.[177]

The Melkite population of Palestine retained almost as much autonomy under the Crusaders as they had under the Muslims. Rural communities and Orthodox neighborhoods in cities were led by prominent laymen with the title *ra'is* (the Arabic term for head or leader). They decided legal issues within the community and represented their coreligionists before the authorities of the kingdom. Local Christians occupied the lower levels of the state's bureaucracy, such as the posts of scribe and dragoman (translator). At the same time, some Melkites managed to reach prominent positions at the court, chiefly as physicians.[178]

Liturgical services in the Melkite communities followed the traditional Byzantine rite. Priests coming from the Arab Melkite milieu were installed by the few Orthodox bishops remaining in Palestine. From liturgical texts of that time, it is clear that during the liturgy the Melkites commemorated the exiled Orthodox patriarchs and ignored the Latin patriarchs of Jerusalem.[179] We may recall the epigraphic inscriptions with the name of the Orthodox patriarch on the walls of monasteries mentioned earlier. Under the conditions of "apartheid," characteristic of the Crusader state, the cultural and everyday alienation between the alien Franks and the indigenous Arab population of the Middle East, the Latins did not seem to be interested in the inner life of their Melkite subjects. Catholic hierarchs were content with a formal expression of submission and payment of tithes by the local Eastern Christian population, while not sufficiently aware of its cultural and religious orientation.[180]

When the Latin patriarchs took over the main shrine of Jerusalem, the Church of the Holy Sepulchre, they nevertheless permitted the Orthodox to worship there to a limited extent, as well as a number of clerics from the non-Chalcedonian churches, an action calculated to induce them to union with Rome. Thus, within the Church of the Holy Sepulchre, there appeared areas belonging to the Armenians, Syrian Jacobites, and Nestorians.

The Principality of Antioch

For almost the entirety of the twelfth century, the Byzantine Empire fought for the return of their former Middle Eastern territories captured by the Crusaders, especially Antioch. Likewise, the emperor considered one of his main objectives to be the restoration of an Orthodox patriarch on the See of Antioch. It was the Latin clergy in particular that formed the core of the anti-Byzantine party in the Principality of Antioch. Several times, Byzantium came close to succeeding. In 1108 Bohemond of Taranto, who had suffered heavy losses from the Greeks at Epirus, pledged to be a vassal of the emperor and promised to return the Orthodox patriarch to Antioch. However, Bohemond's nephew Tancred, who ruled the city, refused to comply with these conditions and, at the time, there were no forces in Byzantium for a military expedition against Antioch. In 1137, the emperor John Comnenus laid siege to the city and forced the prince of Antioch, Raymond, to recognize the empire's suzerainty, but the pope forbade Catholics from serving in

John's army if he attempted to replace the Latin patriarch of Antioch with a Greek. John soon died in 1143, having failed to gain a foothold in Syria. Byzantium's real triumph was Manuel Comnenus's march on Antioch in 1159, when the prince of Antioch, Reynald, realized the complete futility of resistance and went to the imperial camp with an expression of total submission, barefoot and with a rope around his neck. One of the terms of the peace treaty was the prince's obligation to accept an Orthodox patriarch into the city. In 1165, Prince Bohemond III met this condition, and Athanasius I returned to the patriarchal see. The Latin patriarch Aimery left the city in protest and the pope threatened the prince with excommunication. The conflict resolved itself five years later when Athanasius died in an earthquake, buried under the ruins of his church. After the Byzantine Empire's disastrous defeat in the battle against the Seljuks at Myriokefala in 1176, Constantinople's having any influence in Syria was out of the question, and a quarter of a century later, Byzantium itself fell to the Crusaders.

Nevertheless, it was then that an Orthodox patriarchate was once again restored in Antioch. In the early thirteenth century, the count of Tripoli, Bohemund IV, disputed the claim for the Principality of Antioch from Cilician Armenia, which at the time was in union with the Church of Rome. The pope and the Latin patriarch of Antioch Peter took the side of the Armenians. Then, in 1206, Bohemond IV deposed the patriarch and invited the Orthodox primate, Simeon II Abu Shayba, to take his place. Despite the excommunication imposed on Antioch by the Latin patriarch, the citizens supported Bohemond's move, which indicates the significant influence of the Orthodox community in Antioch.

The fate of the patriarchs of Antioch evolved even further and they often became the object of bargaining in disputes between Middle Eastern monarchs. Around 1209 Bohemond reconciled with Rome and forced Simeon to leave the city. Subsequently, Simeon was able to return and stay in Antioch in parallel with the Latin patriarch. In the 1230s, Rome realized the impossibility of directly incorporating Eastern Christians into the Catholic Church and moved to create an autonomous Melkite church structure that would be in union with Rome. Simeon rejected this project, but his successor David, who may have owed his election to the prince of Antioch's court, was inclined to negotiate with the pope in the 1240s. Although the Latin patriarch of Antioch Albert did not welcome the emergence of a parallel hierarch in union with Rome, he nevertheless left David as his deputy when he left for the council of Lyon in 1245. Until 1248, David would be the only patriarch in Antioch. A philo-Catholic sentiment, however, was not generally characteristic of the clergy of Antioch. The following patriarch, Euthymius, refused to recognize the primacy of Rome, for which he was expelled from the city roughly in the late 1250s.[181]

Interregnum (1187–1250)

On July 4, 1187, at the Battle of Hattin, Salah al-Din, the most famous member of the new Ayyubid dynasty that ruled Egypt from 1168 to 1250, destroyed the Crusaders' army and then seized almost the entire territory of the Kingdom of Jerusalem. According to several sources, the Orthodox of the Holy Land welcomed the return of Muslim rule and were even ready to open the gates to Salah al-Din's army. Jerusalem surrendered to the Muslims in the autumn of 1187 and the Frankish population was expelled from the city. After this disaster for the crusading movement, Western European monarchs undertook the Third Crusade to Palestine (1189–1193) but won only a narrow strip along the coast and could not regain the Holy City. The Kingdom of Jerusalem, whose capital moved to Acre, continued to exist for a century, but most of Palestine and Transjordan remained in Muslim hands.

The expulsion of the Latins from Jerusalem gave the Orthodox Church a chance to recover the holy places. The

Byzantine emperor Isaac Angelos negotiated with Salah al-Din for the transfer of the Palestinian shrines into the undivided ownership of the Orthodox Church and for the right of the emperor to appoint the patriarch of Jerusalem. Byzantium's demands were not successful and Salah al-Din retained the prerogative of determining the affiliation of the holy places. In addition to the Orthodox, who regained the Basilica of the Resurrection and a number of other areas of the Holy Sepulchre church complex, the Armenians, Syrian Jacobites, and Nestorians retained possession over their part of the church. Additionally, the Ayyubids set apart areas for their Coptic Egyptian subjects, after which Ethiopians came to Jerusalem. Georgians came to play an increasingly important role within the Orthodox community in Palestine and so they also received their own area in the Church of the Holy Sepulchre. Queen Tamar maintained friendly relations with the Ayyubids and actively funded Georgian monasteries in the Holy Land. In a situation in which the Latins had been expelled from Jerusalem and Byzantium was increasingly weakened, the Georgian Bagratids claimed the role of chief patron of the Orthodox East. Finally, in 1193, after the conclusion of a peace with the Crusaders, the Ayyubids even allowed Latin clergy to worship in the church.[182] In this way, there largely developed the situation that continues to the present day of coexistence and competition in the Holy Sepulchre between Christian denominations whose relations are governed by a non-Christian secular authority.

For unclear reasons, in the late twelfth century, the Orthodox patriarchs were in no hurry to return to the Holy

Land and preferred to stay in Constantinople. The first patriarch to reside in the Holy Land was Euthymius III who escaped from the Byzantine capital after the Crusaders seized it in 1204 and presumably was elected to the patriarchal see already in Jerusalem.

In the thirteenth century, the main target of the Crusaders' onslaught was Egypt, where the Fifth (1218–1221) and Seventh (1248–1250) Crusades were sent. On the eve of the Crusaders' invasion of Egypt, the Patriarch of Alexandria Nicholas I (c. 1220–1235) sought to obtain the favor of the spiritual leader of the Western world, Pope Innocent III, with whom he exchanged a number of friendly letters. At the pope's invitation, a representative of the patriarch attended the Lateran Council of 1215. After the failure of the Fifth Crusade, Nicholas sent Pope Honorius a letter full of complaints about the miseries of Egyptian Christians and pleas for help.[183]

Perhaps the persecution of Christians in Ayyubid territory during the Fifth Crusade is behind the flight of Patriarch of Jerusalem Euthymius III to the Monastery of Sinai, where he died in 1235. It appears that Euthymius maintained ties with the Crusaders on the eve of their campaign. His appeals to Christians to refrain from pilgrimage to Palestine in order not to enrich the Hagarenes with their gifts clearly resonated with the Lateran Council's prohibition of the sale of weapons and ship timber to Egypt.[184]

Despite all this, the European prelates and knights themselves continued to refer to Eastern Christians as heretics. During the Crusader armies' invasion of Egypt, they plundered and massacred the local population, making no distinction between Muslims and Christians. In 1219, after the capture of Damietta, which previously had been the see of an Orthodox metropolitan and a Coptic bishop, the papal legate established a Latin see in the city and annexed Damietta to the possessions of the Latin patriarch of Jerusalem. The same thing happened after the Crusaders captured the city again in 1249. In the Catholic Church in the thirteenth century, the position of Latin patriarch of Alexandria was introduced, although it remained a purely nominal, honorary title.[185]

The Orthodox position in the Middle East dramatically deteriorated in the twelfth and thirteenth centuries, and not solely because of the various pressures from the Latin Crusaders. On the other side of the front, in the Muslim world, the situation of two centuries of continuous jihad against the infidels spawned the rise of fanaticism and intolerance and numerous persecutions against Christians. For example, in 1124, almost all churches in Aleppo were taken away from the Christians and converted into mosques.[186]

During military actions, the chief victims were from the local Christian population. For example, during the fierce fighting between the Crusaders and the Muslims for Edessa from 1144 to 1146, the city changed hands several times and eventually was burned to the ground, with almost all its Christian population annihilated. A contemporary of the events, the Jacobite patriarch and historian Michael the Syrian vividly described the final act of this drama:

> The bodies of priests, deacons, monks, nobles and commoners were piled up in a jumble. But if their

death was terrible, they did not taste the torment
endured by the survivors ... The air was poisoned
by a putrid stench. Assyria [Mesopotamia] was inun-
dated with prisoners ... Around 30,000 died during
the first and second siege [of Edessa]. 16,000 were
taken off into slavery and one thousand were saved.
Not one woman or child survived. They were killed
during the massacres or were led off into captivity in
various lands. Edessa became like a desert."[187]

At the beginning of his reign, the sultan Salah al-Din placed
especially severe restrictions on infidels. In his edicts, Christians were expelled from government posts and they were
required to wear distinctive clothing and not allowed to ride
horses. He launched a number of devastating campaigns
against Christian Nubia.[188] Another surge of Muslim fanaticism swept the Middle East after Salah al-Din's victory over
the Crusaders at Hattin in 1187. "There are no words," wrote
Michael the Syrian, "to express how much damage, injury
and humiliation at the hands of the Muslims has been suffered by Christians in Damascus, Aleppo, Harran, Edessa,
Mardin, Mosul and everywhere under Muslim rule."[189]
After defeating the Crusaders, however, Salah al-Din, to
strengthen his political position, backed away from a policy
of intolerance and returned non-Muslims to the administrative apparatus of Egypt.[190]

New calamities befell the Christians during the Fifth
Crusade. The Copts of Cairo were levied with a heavy collection for military expenditures. The Muslim army destroyed
all the churches along its path to Damietta. In response to

the Crusaders' capture of Damietta, 115 churches were destroyed throughout Egypt.[191]

In 1229, the emperor Frederick Hohenstaufen was able to negotiate with the Ayyubids for the return to the Crusaders of Jerusalem, Bethlehem, and a corridor connecting them to the coast. At the same time, it was stipulated that the Muslim presence in the Holy City would be preserved, in particular in the religious complex on the Temple Mount and that the construction of fortifications in the city would be forbidden. The Franks' hold on Jerusalem was shaky; the Latin patriarch preferred to stay in Acre. In this situation, the position of the Orthodox Church was not changed.

Patriarch Athanasius II of Jerusalem (before 1229–1244), who presumably came from the Balkans, was in close contact with the entire Orthodox world. He corresponded with the patriarch of Constantinople about ritual differences with the Latins and participated in the approval of the autocephaly of the Bulgarian Church in 1235. In 1229 and 1234–1235, the Holy Land was visited by the Serbian archbishop Sava Nemanjić who had close ties of friendship with Patriarch Athanasius and the abbot of Mar Saba Nicholas. The Life of St Sava of Serbia provides us with detailed information about the state of Middle Eastern Orthodoxy and in particular about the monasteries and monks of the first third of the thirteenth century. Sava made generous contributions to the Palestinian monasteries and places of worship and himself founded several monasteries, including a monastery in Acre that was to serve as a hostel for Orthodox pilgrims. The Life repeatedly mentions Athanasius serving the liturgy in the

Church of the Resurrection as well as Sava's founding the Monastery of St John the Theologian on Mount Sion, along with the patriarch and the abbot of Mar Saba, indicated the Orthodox Church's strong position in Jerusalem during the second period of Crusader rule.

From the late 1230s, however, the situation in Palestine changed for the worse. Jerusalem became the object of military confrontation between the Crusaders and the Muslims and switched hands several times. Political instability led to the exodus of a large part of the Christian population of the Holy Land. On August 23, 1244, Jerusalem was stormed by an army of Khwarezmians, allies of the Egyptian sultan. Catholics and Orthodox sought refuge in the Church of the Holy Sepulchre but were slaughtered. Among those who perished was Patriarch Athanasius II, who subsequently was canonized as a martyr by the Church of Jerusalem.[192]

Mongols and Mamluks

Having alienated their potential allies, the Eastern Christians, the Crusaders were doomed to defeat in their struggle with the Islamic world with its far superior military and demographic resources. The final chance to change the political situation in favor of the Christians came in the middle of the thirteenth century with the arrival of the Mongols in the Middle East. The Mongols were for the most part shamanists, but were also familiar with the preachings of Nestorianism and Buddhism and were hostilely disposed toward the Muslims. The last united campaign of the Chingizids,[193] which began under Hülegü in 1256, was intended to crush the Muslim states. Moving from Baghdad to Damascus, the Mongols consistently exterminated Muslims but spared the Christian population. Only during the assault on Aleppo in the autumn of 1259 did Orthodox suffer in the heat of the massacre.[194] Georgia, Cilician Armenia, and the Principality of Antioch recognized the suzerainty of Hülegü Khan. At the insistence of Hülegü, who valued his alliance with the Empire of Nicaea, Prince Bohemond VI of Antioch returned the Orthodox Patriarch Euthymius to the city and sent away the Latin patriarch, for which he was excommunicated by the pope.

On March 1, 1260, the vanguard of the Mongol army, led by Hülegü's close associate, the Nestorian Kitbuqa Noyan, arrived in Damascus. Kitbuqa was accompanied by the king of Cilician Armenia, Hetoum, and Prince Bohemund of Antioch. According to the British Byzantinist Steven Runciman, "The citizens of the ancient capital of the Caliphate saw for the first time for six centuries three Christian potentates ride in triumph through their streets."[195] The Christians welcomed the establishment of the new government. It is symptomatic that the victors turned the Umayyad Mosque into a Christian church. By late summer 1260, the Mongols had completed the subjugation of Syria and most of Palestine but for some reason did not occupy Jerusalem.[196]

At the same time, the Crusaders of the Kingdom of Jerusalem did not perceive the Mongols as allies. There was great prejudice against the invaders among the Europeans. The kingdom was dominated by Venetian merchants who were concerned about the profitable trade with Muslim Egypt. After a local conflict with the Mongols near Sidon, the Christians of Acre entered into an alliance with the Muslims and allowed the army of the Egyptian Mamluks to pass through their territory on their way to the territory of the Mongols.[197]

After the death of the khagan Möngke, Hülegü returned with most of his army to Tabriz to participate in resolving the question of succession in the state of the descendants of

Genghis Khan. The remaining body of Mongols in Syria, headed by the general Kitbuqa Noyan, was defeated on September 3, 1260, in a battle with the Mamluks at ʿAyn Jalut in Galilee. Kitbuqa was captured and executed. At the news of this victory, a pogrom against Christians began in Damascus, the Cathedral of Mart Maryam was burned, and anyone known to have collaborated with the Mongols was killed.[198] The Mamluks concluded an alliance with Hülegü's Muslim opponents, the Anatolian Seljuks and Khan Berke of the Golden Horde; constricted the Mongols with assaults from different directions; and, in a series of military campaigns, were able to drive them out of Syria. Then came the time of reckoning for Hülegü Khan's Christian allies.

In the 1260s the Egyptian sultan Baybars waged a number of successful campaigns against the Crusader states and Cilician Armenia. These wars were accompanied by a demonstrative extermination of infidels: mass executions of Christian prisoners of war and civilians. In the summer of 1266, the Muslim army devastated Cilician Armenia, which never recovered from the blow.

As the Mamluk army was returning from a campaign in Armenia, Baybars ordered that the inhabitants of the large Christian town of Qara, to the south of Homs on the edge of the Qalamun Plateau, be killed, accusing them of banditry and having connections with the Crusaders. Qara, however, was soon populated with Christians once more and became an important center of Syriac-speaking Melkite culture.[199]

On May 12, 1268, Baybars's army appeared at the walls of Antioch. At that time Prince Bohemond VI was in Tripoli and his constable Simon Mansel led the defense of the city. The garrison was too small to protect the walls and Mansel was soon captured during a raid. The people of the city were able to repel the first attack, but on May 18, the Mamluks launched a general assault on all sections of the walls and broke through the defenses on one side. The ensuing carnage shocked even Muslim chroniclers. Tens of thousands of the city's inhabitants were killed and the rest were sold into slavery. The city was burned and left completely desolate.[200]

The Orthodox patriarch Euthymius had once again been exiled by Prince Bohemond of Antioch in 1263 (enraging Hülegü Khan, who continued to be focused on an alliance with the Orthodox world) and at the time of the city's fall was in Byzantium. After the events of 1268, the patriarchs of Antioch never again returned to their former capital.[201]

The weakening of the threat from the east following the unsuccessful Mongol invasion of Syria in the fall of 1281 freed the hands of the Mamluks to crush the remnants of the Frankish possessions along the coast. The county of Tripoli, in turn, suffered from internal unrest.[202] A split also took place among the Lebanese Maronite Christians, traditional allies of the Franks. The Maronites were a confederation of tribes ruled by their own *sheikhs-muqaddams* who had rather divergent interests. While coastal communities led by the patriarch Irmiya al-Dimilsawi (1282–1297) remained loyal to the Roman Catholic Church and the counts of Tripoli, some monastic leaders elected their own patriarch, Luqa al-Bnahrani, and fell out of union with Rome, taking with them the tribes of the highland district of Bsharri. It was this region that in 1283 was raided by allies of the Mamluk sultan: a Turkmen army that crossed Mount Lebanon through passes from the Bekaa Valley. One by one, the mountainous Maronite villages fell to the Muslims' blows; their population was partly slaughtered and partly taken captive. The patriarch Luqa was also taken captive and his subsequent fate is unknown.[203]

In mid-March 1289, the Mamluk sultan Qalawun marched on Tripoli from Damascus. He was accompanied on the campaign by many Muslim religious authorities from Damascus and Jerusalem, who were tasked with maintaining the morale of the troops. Nineteen ballistas and mangonels were brought along for the siege. Tripoli was fired upon continuously by the mangonels and its walls were breached. The collapse of two towers in the southern part of the fortifications and the departure of Venetian and Genoese troops from the city prompted Qalawun to give the order for a general assault on Tripoli, which took place on April 26, 1289.[204]

Al-Nuwayri reports that the sultan at first wanted to keep the city and leave a garrison there. He was no doubt dissuaded from this by the threat of a new landing by the Franks along the coast and their return to Tripoli. The fear of Crusader revenge—by no means groundless—was a preoccupation of Muslim society during the Mamluk period. As a result, Qalawun ordered that the conquered city be destroyed. A new settlement, inheriting the name Tripoli, was established three kilometers from the sea, at the foot of the castle of Mont Pelerin (Qal'at Sanjil), on the bank of the Qadisha River. The Lebanese Orthodox reacted emotionally to the fall of Tripoli. Almost immediately after these events, Sulayman al-Ashluhi, a native of the no longer extant village of Ashluh on the Akkar Plateau, composed an elegy in verse on the demise of the city, a rare monument of the literary activity of Melkites in the rural hinterland.[205]

The successful capture of Tripoli led the Mamluks to the idea of a final blow to the Crusaders. In 1291, under Qalawun's son and successor al-Ashraf Khalil (1290–1293), the Muslims crushed Acre, the capital of the Crusader kingdom, and afterwards seized the Franks' remaining cities along the coast—Beirut, Tyre, Tartus, and others—without a fight. After the Crusaders' expulsion, the Mamluks long anticipated a new landing by European knights. To aggravate the situation, the Muslim authorities destroyed most of the coastal cities and fortifications, such as Ashkelon, Caesarea, and Acre.

Following the expulsion of the Franks, the Mamluks drew their swords against the "heretical" communities of Mount Lebanon, who could have acted as allies of the Crusaders in the event of a new landing by them. The blow fell upon the Druze, Shiites, and Christians inhabiting the mountainous district of Keserwan to the northeast of Beirut. The first campaign against Keserwan in 1292 ended in failure—the commander of the army, the emir Baydar, suffered a series of defeats and retreated having achieved nothing. His detractors spread rumors that he had allowed himself to be bribed by the elders of Lebanese tribes and deliberately lost the campaign. The Mongol invasion of Syria in 1301 was, as before, accompanied by attacks by Lebanese highlanders on the retreating Muslim troops. After driving away the Mongols, the Mamluks launched a large-scale punitive expedition in Keserwan in 1302 and, following a new uprising by the local inhabitants in 1305, they carried out radical ethnic cleansing there, from which many Christian villages and monasteries suffered.[206] It would only be in the sixteenth century that Keserwan would again be densely populated by Maronites.

The era of the Crusades was a turning point in the history of Middle Eastern Christianity. Over two hundred years, Christians, who in the eleventh century formed almost half the population in Syria and Palestine, were nearly destroyed to the extent such that they were surviving as merely vestigial ethnoreligious groups.

The Century of Persecution

By the end of the thirteenth century, all of Syria had been incorporated into the Mamluk Sultanate. For nearly three centuries, the fate of the Melkites was tied to this state, which became the political and religious center of the Muslim world and the center of Arab culture.

For the first half-century of their reign, the Mamluks were in permanent confrontation with the Mongols over control of Syria. The last attack on Damascus by a descendant of Hülegü, Khan Ghazan, was recorded in 1303. The subsequent disintegration of the state of Hülegü's descendants secured for the Mamluk state a century of peace, interrupted only by conflicts within the ruling elite and coastal raids by European corsairs. The Mamluks waged a number of campaigns of conquest in Eastern Anatolia and Nubia. In 1315, the Mamluk army put Malatya to fire and the sword. In a few blows, Cilician Armenia was finished. The last king of Cilicia, besieged in his capital, surrendered to the Mamluks in 1375.

In comparison with previous Muslim dynasties, the religious policy of the Mamluks was distinguished by a much greater intolerance of *dhimmis*. Foremost among the reasons for this intolerance was the psychological effects of the Crusades and the anti-Christian sentiment that they caused, which constantly was stirred up by the sermons of Muslim theologians and found many supporters among the common people who were dissatisfied with the dominance of Christian officials. The long standoff with Hülegü's dynasty, which openly patronized the Christians and relied on allied troops from Georgia and Cilician Armenia, also may have played a role. The loss by Muslim merchants of their standing in Mediterranean trade stimulated the migration of the Muslim middle class into the area of state administration, from which they first needed to push out the Christians. This included the dismissal of non-Muslim officials from public service, the introduction of distinctive clothing for *dhimmis*, various domestic constraints, and the destruction of newly built churches.[207] In contrast to the era of al-Hakim, when the persecution of *dhimmis* was inspired by the government, in the late Middle Ages, the initiative came from religious circles and the masses—what would now be called "civil society," which sometimes was able to exert effective pressure on the Mamluk military oligarchy. The spirit of intolerance, characteristic of the Mamluk era, was embodied in the treatises and sermons of the authoritative Hanbalite theologians Ibn Taymiyya (1263–1328), Ibn Qayyim al-Jawziyya (1292–1350), and Ibn al-Naqqash (d. 1362), who had an enormous influence on the masses of ordinary people.

The Coptic community of Egypt in the early Mamluk era was dynamic and thriving, with a strong sense of identity embodied in an active literary life. At the same time, the relative proportion of Copts in the country's population continued to fall, while the proportion of the Muslim community increased, which, among other factors, took place with the influx from the outside to the Nile Valley because of the settling of the Bedouin population. The percentage of unmarried clergy among Christians still remained high. In thirteenth-century Egypt, there were about fifty Coptic dioceses and ninety monasteries. Additionally, it is believed that in the Christian milieu, artificial birth control and various methods of contraception were practiced. These phenomena have been well studied on the basis of the example of late-medieval Egypt. But if, after the Black Death, birth control was encouraged by poverty and uncertainty about the future, the motives of the Copts in the thirteenth century were quite different: maintaining a high standard of living within a small, close-knit community. The Copts' wealth and their awareness of a special intracommunal solidarity provoked the hostility of their Muslim environment. Under the Mamluks, the demographic balance swung sharply toward the Muslims, ushering in what historians call "the century of persecutions."[208]

The chronological range of this period is defined in different ways. In our view, it is proper to speak of a time period between the reign of Baybars (1260–1277) and the Alexandrian Crusade in 1365. The Christians of the Mamluk state were subjected to a fierce persecution about once every twenty years, which led to a severe crisis in the Coptic and other Christian communities.

The wars with the Mongols and the Crusaders exerted maximal stress on the economy and were accompanied by a ruthless extraction of funds from the tax-paying population, primarily non-Muslims. Starting in 1261, Christians paid an additional tax for military needs that was only cancelled in 1279, when Qalawun ascended the throne. Traditional sharia regulations regarding everyday discrimination were renewed, including that Christians wear blue turbans and be banned from using horses and mules. At the same time, *dhimmis* continued to occupy important positions in the administration, an example of which is the biography of the Coptic scholar al-Makin (1205–1273), a former official in the military, first in Cairo and then in Damascus.

At the same time, the Muslim majority regarded *dhimmis* as the fifth column of external enemies. Fires in Cairo, which became more frequent in the spring of 1265, were blamed on the maliciousness of Christians avenging the destruction of Palestinian churches during Baybars's campaign against Caesarea and Arsuf. Returning to Cairo in early summer, Baybars accused the Christian and Jewish elites of political disloyalty, which meant the nullification of the "protection" guaranteed to *dhimmis* by sharia. The sultan ordered that the heads of non-Muslim communities be burned in ditches filled with kindling. Among those condemned was the Coptic patriarch John VII. At the last moment, however, Baybars yielded to the pleas of his entourage and commuted the death sentence to an obligation by the patriarch to pay on behalf of his community the astronomical sum of five hundred thousand dinars in installments of fifty thousand dinars a year. This money was paid for many years by "beating" the funds out of the Coptic archons. Some of them died from torture and many others converted to Islam in order to avoid the battery.[209]

Discriminatory measures against *dhimmis* were continued during the reign of Sultan Qalawun (1279–1290) and periodically (in 1280 and 1290) individual departments or the entire bureaucracy were purged of Christian officials. These steps had little effect judging by the fact that at the beginning of the reign of Qalawun's successor, Sultan al-Ashraf Khalil (1290–1293), Christians dominated all administrative structures and ceased to comply with the restrictions imposed on them.

This situation provoked the Muslim lower classes and religious leaders. It is characteristic that the majority of religious persecutions under the Mamluk state began not at the initiative of the authorities but under the pressure of public opinion and, often, the threat of mass riots. Thus, in 1293, the defiant behavior of the Coptic official ʿAyn al-Jazal provoked anti-Christian outbursts by the Cairo mob, the plundering of Christian homes, and the murder of non-Muslims. The sultan attempted to put a stop to the pogroms while also issuing a decree prohibiting non-Muslims from government service and ordering the conversion of Coptic officials to Islam. Under the threat of execution, the majority of Christian secretaries converted to Islam.

The next purge of non-Muslims from the bureaucracy and resumption of everyday restrictions on *dhimmis* occurred in 1301. Chronicles connect this persecution to the

presence in Cairo of a Maghrebi vizier who was shocked by
the dominance of Christians and convinced the emir Baybars al-Jashnakir, the de facto ruler during the minority
of the sultan al-Nasir Muhammad, to bring the status of
non-Muslims into accordance with the provisions of sharia.
Perhaps the anti-Christian measures were also connected
to the next round in the struggle between the Mongols
and Mamluks over Syria and the temporary occupation of
Damascus by the Hülegüids: war hysteria stimulated the
growth of religious piety. The Coptic patriarch and the
heads of the Christian and Jewish communities were summoned to the council of emirs and Muslim jurists where they
pledged to abide by the restrictions on clothing and everyday life prescribed for *dhimmis*: the bans on riding horses,
bearing arms, employing Muslims for hard labor, religious
processions, and the use of clappers in churches. The humil-
iating restrictions and a ban on accepting non-Muslims into
government service prompted some Christian officials to
convert to Islam. The injunction that Christians not con-
struct buildings higher than the homes of Muslims provoked
pogroms against churches and the shops of *dhimmis* in Cairo,
Alexandria, and Fayyum. Churches in Egypt remained
closed for several more years, until the authorities abolished
the anti-Christian rules at the insistence of Byzantine and
Catalan embassies.[210]

Sultan al-Nasir Muhammad, who was the sole ruler of
Egypt from 1310 to 1341, made extensive use of Christians
in the bureaucracy. The second wealthiest and most influential person in the state was the manager of the sultan's

properties, Karim al-Din al-Kabir, a Copt who had converted to Islam as an adult in the first years of the fourteenth
century and continued to patronize Christian officials. The
financial and administrative reforms conducted by Karim
al-Din in the 1310s left many loopholes for *dhimmis* to avoid
paying the *jizya*, something that was regarded in Muslim
circles as a conspiracy against the state by Coptic bureaucrats. The emirs were unhappy with Karim al-Din's absolute power. Perhaps these internal political contradictions
were reflected in the wave of anti-Christian riots, unprecedented in scope and organization, which swept across Egypt
on May 8, 1321, leading to the destruction of sixty churches
and monasteries from Aswan to Damietta. In June of that
year, the city of Cairo was engulfed in catastrophic fires
that were blamed on Christian arsonists taking revenge
for the recent pogroms. Several dozen Orthodox and Coptic monks and laymen were executed on charges of arson.
Seeing the increase in anti-Christian sentiments and fearing
serious unrest, the sultan issued a decree for the resumption
of everyday restrictions on *dhimmis*, the dismissal of Coptic
officials, and the doubling of the *jizya*.[211] Popular discontent
was primarily directed against Karim al-Din, the symbol of
Christian influence in government structures. In 1323, the
all-powerful minister was sent into exile and subsequently
killed. Al-Nasir Muhammad, however, continued to employ
the service of Coptic officials and recent converts to Islam
from a Coptic background. The position of Karim al-Din
in the 1330s was inherited by another recent convert from
Christianity, Sharaf al-Din al-Nashw, who aroused universal

hatred with his exactions and tyranny. In the Coptic historiography, al-Nashw appears as a ruthless oppressor of Christians and his execution in 1339 is attributed to the prayers of
the patriarch Benjamin II.[212]

The turning point in the history of the Coptic community is the persecution of August 1354, provoked by the
scandalous luxury and arrogance of Christian officials.
Under pressure from public opinion, the authorities rein-
stated sharia restrictions on non-Muslims and launched a
campaign to remove Copts from the bureaucracy. A new
and extremely important element of the repression was the
confiscation of twenty-five thousand *feddans* (ten thousand
hectares) of church lands. As before, the Muslim mob inter-
preted the sultan's decrees as permission to attack Christians
and churches. In Cairo and the surrounding district, five
churches were looted and destroyed. Copts converted en
masse to Islam in both cities and rural areas. According to
al-Maqrizi, the majority of churches in Upper Egypt were
destroyed and rebuilt as mosques. Even adopting Islam did
not spare newly converted officials from suspicion: they were
required to regularly visit the mosque and cease contact with
Christian relatives.[213]

The brief capture of Alexandria by the king of Cyprus,
Pierre de Lusignan, in October 1365 and the support for
the Crusaders by local Christians provoked a new wave of
repression. The force of the blow fell upon European monks
and merchants living in Mamluk territory as well as upon
the Orthodox of Syria and Palestine. Patriarch Lazarus of
Jerusalem was thrown into prison, subjected to beatings and

threatened with execution. The Church of the Holy Sepulchre and many other churches were closed and sealed off and the priests of Jerusalem were imprisoned. Patriarch Pachomius of Antioch aroused the suspicions of the Muslim authorities and was deposed. In June of 1366, the Melkites were permitted to choose a new patriarch, but he was ordered to remain in Damascus under the tight control of the Mamluk emir. Christians were ordered to contribute a quarter of their property for the ransom of captured Muslims and the construction of a fleet. Egyptian monasteries did not escape targeted looting. In Coptic hagiographic literature there are references to arrests and beatings of monks during Mamluk raids on desert monasteries. In the summer or fall of 1366, a Byzantine embassy secured an end to the persecution and the freedom of Patriarch Lazarus, though outbreaks of persecution continued even longer. After an attack on Tripoli by the Cypriot fleet in early 1367, the Mamluks set the Maronite patriarch Jibra'il on fire.[214]

It seems that the situation of Christian officials in the Mamluk bureaucracy was seriously undermined. Nevertheless, Christian scribes still occasionally appear in sources of the late fourteenth and early fifteenth centuries working in the administration of sultans and emirs, in addition to recent converts to Islam from a Coptic background who reached high positions in the government. Around a quarter of the clans of officials who made up the highest echelons of the Egyptian bureaucracy in the fifteenth century had a Christian background, but these bureaucrats were already second- or third-generation Muslims, fully integrated into Arab

Muslim culture. It is characteristic that the Muslim environment did not accept Islamized Copts as fully Muslim. Converts were not allowed to practice jurisprudence or to study or teach the religious sciences, but rather they were employed exclusively in the bureaucratic and financial administration. Campaigns to dismiss or Islamize Christian officials were relatively rare over the course of the fifteenth century, occurring in 1419, 1422, and 1463, which indirectly indicates the decline of Christians' role in the state bureaucracy. Alongside secretaries, other elite groups of Christians—physicians and money-changers—were subject to persecution. Thus, in 1448, by decree of the sultan, *dhimmi* physicians were prohibited from providing services to Muslims.

The greatest shock to the countries of the Levant was the Black Death pandemic of 1347–1348, which wiped out as much as a third of the population.[215] A series of crop failures and famines in the late fourteenth and early fifteenth centuries, followed by new outbreaks of the plague, gave rise to a surge of apocalyptic sentiment in Egyptian society. Droughts and epidemics were seen as God's punishment for the decline of Muslim piety. Natural disasters provoked campaigns against social vices, including trade in wine, during which Christian neighborhoods were searched and any wine found was destroyed. Time and again, sharia injunctions for everyday discrimination against Christians were renewed: fixed sizes for turbans, blue clothing, the prohibition against riding horses, etc. Similar measures were introduced in 1417, 1419, 1442, and 1463; the very frequency of these decrees, however, testifies to their lack of effectiveness, something that is also confirmed by Arab Muslim authors.[216]

According to some authors, the persecution by the Mamluks led to the same sharp reduction in the number of Christians in Egypt as had the wars of the Crusaders in Syria and Palestine and the anti-Christian persecutions after the conversion of the Hülegü's descendants to Islam in Iran and Mesopotamia in 1295.[217] With the conversion to Islam of the Coptic cultural elite, there came a sharp cultural decline among the remaining part of the Christian community. Literary creativity and iconography ceased and monasteries became extinct.

The Second Crisis
of the Christian East

The social and political discrimination against Christians was exacerbated by a crisis in agriculture in the Middle East brought about by environmental factors as well as the expansion of Bedouin tribes. In the thirteenth century, the invasion of nomads, accompanied by the destruction of the irrigation network in the Jazira (Upper Mesopotamia), converted millions of hectares of fertile land in the Euphrates, Khabur, and Balikh basins into pastureland. Agriculture would only be revived in the region in the 1920s. It was in the thirteenth century that Raqqa (Kallinikos), once the favorite residence of the caliphs, which Arab geographers called one of the best parts of the world, was abandoned by its inhabitants.[218] At this time Sergiopolis (Rusafa), a Christian city surrounded by desert and living off the caravan trade, died out.[219] By the thirteenth century, there is mention of the desolation of the Palmyra oasis, where agriculture was maintained through a complex system of underground channels that since then had been abandoned and dried out.[220] About the time of the destruction of Antioch by Baybars, the largest Syrian monastery, Mar Samʿan on the Black Mountain, came to be uninhabited. Transjordan, whose military and strategic importance increased during the Muslims' wars with the Crusaders, again entered into a period of decline and depopulation after the Crusader states were crushed. In a geographic description from 1300, it is reported that "only ruins remain" of Amman.[221] The exodus of the Christian population from Southern Palestine and Transjordan continued under pressure from the desert. The patriarchs gradually lost contact with Christians living in remote mountain and desert areas, and the territory in which church institutions operated continued shrinking.

An exception to this general backdrop of decline was the rise of a number of Christian urban centers in Transjordan, especially Kerak and Shawbak. Kerak was one of the most important administrative centers of the Mamluk state. Both cities had large Christian populations. Because of this, in 1301 the governor of Kerak even refused to enforce the sultan's decree on the distinctive clothing of *dhimmis*, in as far as they did not need to be differentiated by them.[222] Many Sinaite monks came from Shawbak, including the monastery's bishop Arsenius al-Shawbaki (c. 1285–1293), who is mentioned in a number of Arabic and Greek colophons.[223] A famous Greco-Arabic Psalter was copied in 1406 by Metropolitan Joachim of Shawbak, commissioned by Sheikh Yuhanna al-Shawbaki.[224] Scholars have even identified a particular Christian medical school of Kerak in the thirteenth and fourteenth centuries, the best representatives of which were authors of medical treatises and court physicians to the Mamluk elites.[225]

A similar process of nomadic expansion took place throughout the Anatolian Plateau after Manzikert. Inner Anatolia is equally suited for agriculture and for cattle. Nomadic Turks simply pushed a significant portion of the agricultural population out of the interior valleys and plateaus, which were now converted into pastures. Christians survived only in coastal areas protected by wooded ridges—in Cilicia, Bithynia, and Pontus—as well as in the rocky canyons of Cappadocia. With the destruction of the agricultural way of life, the cities also fell into decline, as they depended on the receipt of products from the rural districts. The subsequent war finished off the Christian population of the cities, which had no place from which to replenish the demographic losses.

Thus, for example, in 1315 the Mamluks seized Malatya and took its entire population into captivity. After that, the metropolitan's see was moved from the city to a monastery located 90 kilometers southeast of Erzincan (Akilisene) and the metropolitan of Malatya himself was appointed by a decision of the Synod of Constantinople to supervise the dioceses of Neocaesarea, Erzincan, and Kemah. This means first of all that in these areas there were no bishops at that time and, second, that there was no longer any possibility for a church hierarchy to exist in the area of Malatya.[226] In 1317, the inhabitants of Amida (Diyabakir) rebelled against the Artuqid emir who ruled Upper Mesopotamia. A punitive expedition killed many of the Christians of Amida, who were led by the Syrian Jacobite bishop, and the cathedral was burned.[227]

Timur's[228] campaigns at the end of the fourteenth century, with their famous scorched-earth tactics and skull pyramids, were a deadly milestone in the fate of Near Eastern Christianity. After that, the Christian population in Southern and Central Mesopotamia disappeared forever. Churches and monasteries were razed, treasure troves of books perished, and cultural traditions were broken. Muslims suffered no less during these disasters (although some of Timur's actions had an emphatic anti-Christian character), but their greater vitality and dominance in the region allowed the Muslim community to regenerate. Even before then, Mesopotamian Christianity had been in a state of serious decline. Throughout the fourteenth century, the Nestorian community diminished and dioceses disappeared even in large cities, such as Baghdad, Tabriz, and Maragha.[229] The Christians who survived Timur's invasion fled north into the mountains between Lakes Van and Urmia. There, among the warlike Kurdish tribes, the Nestorians forgot their old urban culture, regressed in their development, and reverted to an archaic culture.

The Christians of Eastern Anatolia also suffered serious losses. At Timur's order, all the inhabitants of Amida, including the Christians, were burned in an enormous bonfire. In Tur 'Abdin on the watershed of the Tigris and Euphrates, local Christians were hunted down and those hiding in caves were literally smoked out.[230] The Christians of Sivas were killed when the city was captured in 1400. In 1402, Timur ordered all the churches of Erzincan destroyed.[231] Almost all the sees of Eastern Anatolia disappeared from the Notitia of the Church of Constantinople during the fourteenth century. The remnants of the Christian population, cut off from the church hierarchy and literary culture, gradually lost their religious traditions and assimilated to the syncretistic beliefs of the Sufi brotherhoods.

Then, during the second half of the fourteenth century, Turkic tribes settled in the "ecological niche" of Anatolian Orthodoxy. At the same time, it seems, there was a continued demographic expansion of Armenians in Eastern Anatolia, who, for some reason, were less affected by the decline gripping the Christian East.[232] The impression is that between the late fourteenth and sixteenth century ecclesiastical jurisdiction over many areas of Eastern Anatolia passed from the Patriarchate of Constantinople to the Patriarchate of Antioch.

The persecution of 1354 is thought to have delivered a fatal blow to the position of the Coptic community. The conversion of a significant proportion of the archons to Islam and the confiscation of church lands undermined the church's chief sources of income. The Copts' cultural decline is evidenced by the cessation of the production of icons and the attenuation of theological thought. The last Copto-Arabic ecclesiastical writer, Ibn Kabar, who compiled a series of encyclopedic works about theology, law, history, and philology, died in 1334. His works summarized the evolution of the Copts' culture. The last historian of Coptic background (who nevertheless fully embraced Arabo-Muslim culture), Mufaddal ibn Abi al-Fada'il, died after 1341. Thereafter followed centuries of creative lethargy among Egyptian Christians.

From the time of the Arab conquest to the beginning of the Mamluk period, the number of diocesan sees of the

Coptic Church had remained almost unchanged at around fifty. After the mid-fourteenth century, however, information about bishops and dioceses almost disappears. The next nearly complete information of this type dates to 1598. It appears from it that during these two and a half centuries the number of dioceses had decreased to two dozen.[233]

Then, in the fourteenth and fifteenth centuries, the Christian state and civilization of Nubia was extinguished. After losing a military confrontation with the Mamluks, the ruling dynasty of the Nubian kingdom of Makuria became a vassal of Cairo and later converted to Islam. The disappearance of Nubian Christianity cannot, however, be explained by external military pressure from its Muslim neighbors alone. Of some hundred and fifty Nubian churches examined by archaeologists, only about half a dozen were converted to mosques or deliberately destroyed, while the rest were simply abandoned. A large role was played by the influx of Arabized nomadic tribes from neighboring deserts starting in the twelfth century, possibly prompted by certain environmental, climatic, or demographic factors. For a long time, Nubian kings were able to restrain Muslim Egypt's onslaught south of the First Cataract with relative success, but in the end they were unable to withstand the spontaneous infiltration of nomads along the entire perimeter of the valley. The Christian population along the banks of the Nile came to be divided into isolated islands in a sea of nomadic tribes. The incapacity of the state, which was prepared to enter into alliances with the nomads and to adopt Islam, led to the demoralization of the indigenous population and its eventual assimilation to the mass of Islamized outsiders.

Middle Eastern Monasticism
of the Mamluk Period

Many monasteries were destroyed during the wars between the Muslims and the Crusaders. In 1183 the Orthodox monastery on Mount Tabor was attacked and the same befell the Monastery of St Euthymius in 1187.[234] The destruction of Antioch by Baybars in 1268 was accompanied by the destruction of the surrounding monasteries and the death of the multiethnic monastic republic of the Black Mountain, the main spiritual center of Syrian Orthodoxy.

As a Muslim spiritual challenge to the monasteries of the Judean Desert, the sultans established in that region the Sufi lodge of Nabi Musa. During its construction, several dozen nearby monastic cells were destroyed. Baybars transferred to its endowment vast lands in the Jordan Valley, which, as it seems, previously belonged to Christian monasteries. Other villages, granted to Mar Saba by the Kingdom of Jerusalem, are also mentioned in documents of the fourteenth century as being Muslim endowments.[235] Thus, many monasteries lost their landholdings in Palestine and were now dependent on alms coming from Christian countries.

The number of monasteries in the Judean Desert steadily decreased. After the twelfth century, there is no mention of the Monastery of St John Chrysostom by Jericho. The latest evidence for the existence of the Lavra of St Chariton is from an Arabic manuscript copied there in 1223. Over the ruins of the Monastery of Kalamon grew, in the thirteenth century, the Arab village of Hajla, which was later abandoned under pressure from the Bedouins. It seems that Sava Nemanjić in the 1230s was the last of the pilgrims and writers who visited and endowed the monasteries of St Theodosius and St Euthymius. In the 1370s the Russian archimandrite Agrefeny found only ruins on the site of the Lavra of St Theodosius. He is also the last to mention the Monastery of Koziba. The Monastery of St Gerasimus, still active at the time of Ignatius of Smolensk's pilgrimage in 1395, was abandoned by the time the next Russian monk, Zosima, visited Palestine in 1420–1421. Around the same time, if not before, the monastery on the Mountain of Temptation vanished. Zosima was the last to visit the Monastery of St John the Baptist, the largest in the Jordan Valley; later pilgrims in the 1480s described it as a bandits' lair.[236]

The last monastery remaining in the desert was Mar Saba, which long played an important role in the Patriarchate of Jerusalem. The Lavra had metochia in Jerusalem and other parts of Palestine and even abroad. In some sources, the Lavra's abbot appears as a figure almost equal to the patriarch.[237]

The reduction of the Christian population of Palestine meant that in place of monks of Arab origin there came an increasing number of monks from the Balkans and the Caucasus. As a result, the monasteries lost their Arab character and were "uprooted" from the local soil.[238]

In general, Middle Eastern monasticism of the Mamluk era is distinguished by its exceptional ethnic diversity. Here we can see a certain symbiosis among Greeks, Arabs, Georgians, and Slavs that is best represented in the Monastery of St Catherine on Mount Sinai. The monks of Sinai produced hundreds of manuscripts in whose colophons appear Arabs from Egypt, Palestine, Transjordan, and Syria, as well as Greeks from Asia Minor, the islands, and other regions.[239] The most famous of the monks of St Catherine during the Mamluk era, Gregory the Sinaite (1275–1346), a Greek from Smyrna, was one of the founders of Byzantine hesychasm.[240] Among the brothers of Sinai, there were compact groups of Serbian and Georgian monks.[241]

The monasteries of the Judean Desert had the same international flavor. In this case, the Arab element in the milieu of Palestinian monasticism had grown noticeably weaker. In contrast to two known Arabic manuscripts from Mar Saba during the thirteenth to the fifteenth centuries, copied in 1247, eleven Greek manuscripts have been preserved, copied by monks of Mar Saba, as well as a lengthy colophon written in Greek by the abbot Ioannicius in 1334. Even Greek poet-theologians were living in the monastery at the turn of the thirteenth to the fourteenth century, perhaps including Nilus, author of the poetic diptychs of the Church of Jerusalem. Additionally, in his pilgrimage, St Sava of Serbia mentions groups of Georgian and Russian monks among the brethren of Mar Saba.[242]

On the basis of extant manuscripts of the thirteenth and fourteenth centuries from the Monastery of St John the Theologian, it is possible to draw a conclusion about the mixed Greek and Arab composition of its inhabitants.[243]

Of all the monks of foreign origin in the Holy Land during the Ayyubid and Mamluk periods, the most prominent are the Georgians. The Mamluk elite, which was largely of Caucasian origin, was interested in maintaining friendly relations with Georgia, from which came the main flow of slaves to replenish the Mamluk army. Additionally, in the twelfth and thirteenth centuries, Georgia was a fairly serious force to be reckoned with among the states of Asia Minor. Georgian kings actively patronized Palestinian Orthodoxy and donated large sums to the Georgian monasteries and pilgrimage infrastructure of the Holy Land. According to testimony from the thirteenth century, magnificent caravans of Georgian pilgrims were allowed to pass to Jerusalem free of duty by the Muslim authorities.[244]

Georgia's alliance with the Mongols in the second half of the thirteenth century, however, greatly complicated the situation of Georgians in Palestine. Around 1268 or 1269, the sultan Baybars turned the Georgian Monastery of the Holy Cross into a Sufi lodge (zawiya). The monastery's abbot, Luke, attempted to protest and was killed. It was only after the end of the series of wars between the Mamluks and the Mongols that the Egyptian sultan, yielding to requests from Georgian and Byzantine embassies in 1305–1306 or 1310–1311, returned the monastery to the Georgians and revoked a number of discriminatory measures directed at Christians.[245]

In the fourteenth century, the Georgians founded or restored many monasteries in and around Jerusalem, including the monasteries of St Thekla, St Catherine, St Basil the Great, St Nicholas, St John the Evangelist on Mount Sion, St Demetrius, and others. The monasteries owned considerable properties, including several villages. The Georgian kings founded the village of Malk and populated it with Georgian colonists who were to support and maintain the monasteries. Later, the villagers were assimilated to their Arab environment and converted to Islam.[246]

Alongside the Georgians, the Serbian monastic community played an increasingly prominent role in Palestine. With his visits to the Middle East, Sava Nemanjić inaugurated an era of close contacts between the South Slavs and the Patriarchate of Jerusalem. Hierarchs of the Serbian Church, some of whom, like Sava, also visited the Holy Land, attempted to transfer the liturgical and monastic tradition of Palestine onto Balkan soil and even imitated the architectural motifs of churches and monasteries of the Holy Land in their church construction. In the early fourteenth century, the Serbian king Stefan Uroš II founded the Monastery of the Archangel Michael in Jerusalem and populated it with Slavic monks. Subsequent rulers of Serbia consistently patronized the Serbian monastic community of Jerusalem. It held one of the most influential places among the Christian communities of the Holy City and, in particular, had its own altar at the Church of the Holy Sepulchre. The destruction of Serbian statehood in the middle of the fourteenth century naturally led to a crisis of the Slavic monastic settlements of the Eastern Mediterranean. It is noteworthy that the Monastery of the Archangel Michael became deserted shortly before 1479 because of an outbreak of the plague and the donations sent to it from the treasury in Dubrovnik by agreement with the old Serbian kings were instead redirected to Hilandar, the center of Serbian monasticism on Mount Athos.[247]

The Melkites and Byzantium

Although monasticism in the Holy Land during the Mamluk period was predominantly of non-Arab origin and parish priests were undoubtedly Arab, the ethnic composition of the upper hierarchy of the Church of Jerusalem is less clear. Many historians (Chrysostomos Papadopoulos, Steven Runciman, Joseph Nasrallah) assume a priori that the patriarchs and bishops of Mamluk Palestine were Arabs who bore Greek names only as a matter of tradition.[248] This claim goes back to the historical writings of seventeenth-century Patriarch of Jerusalem Dositheos Notaras but is not supported by sufficient evidence.

The names of the patriarchs of Jerusalem from the thirteenth to the fifteenth centuries are known but, as Richard B. Rose correctly remarks, we do not know whether these people spoke Greek, Arabic, or Syriac and, more generally, whether it would have been of any significance during this era.[249] On the other hand, the Church of Jerusalem had a close relationship with Byzantium, to the point that some patriarchs of the fourteenth century were installed and deposed by the decision of the Synod of Constantinople and the emperors. The patriarchs of Jerusalem often visited Byzantium and lived there for years. It can be argued with a high degree of confidence that a number of patriarchs of Jerusalem were of Greek origin or belonged to Greek-speaking culture and maintained close ties with Byzantium. Additionally, some primates of the Holy City most likely did come from an Arab milieu.

Patriarch Gregory I of Jerusalem (before 1274–1291) was actively involved in the ecclesio-political struggle in Byzantium after the Union of Lyon in 1274. The patriarch acted as a mediator in negotiations between Bulgaria and Egypt for an alliance against Emperor Michael Palaeologus, the union's initiator. Although the planned alliance was never formed, Gregory for his own part denounced Michael's church policy and prompted the Byzantine theologian George Moschobar to compose a treatise against the Latins.[250] Gregory's successor, Patriarch Sophronius (1291–1303), was probably of Egyptian Arab origin.[251]

When Patriarch Athanasius III (1303–1316), during an absence from Palestine around 1308, was deposed through the intrigues of a member of the Palestinian clergy, Gabriel Vroulas, he submitted a complaint to the Byzantine emperor and the Synod of Constantinople. The emperor's envoys who were sent to Palestine to verify the allegations leveled against Athanasius deposed him in absentia and elevated Gabriel to the patriarchate. Athanasius was only able to regain his see by appearing before the emperor in person and convincing him of his cause.[252] This episode provides a vivid illustration of the strength of the ties and the degree of dependence of the clergy of Jerusalem on Byzantium at that time.

However, the next patriarch, Gregory II (c. 1316–1334), was elected by the local clergy and the patriarch of Constantinople was simply informed of this by his letter. An Arabic note by the patriarch from 1322 appears in an old Greek gospel book.[253] Someone who wrote in Arabic in the margins of a Greek book clearly had to have been an Arab.

The greatest figure in the history of the Church of Jerusalem in the fourteenth century was Patriarch Lazarus. Elected to the patriarchate by the Palestinian clergy around 1334, he went to Constantinople to be confirmed and officially consecrated. Lazarus's rival Gerasimus also went to the capital of the empire and made various accusations against Lazarus, and so an imperial embassy was sent to Jerusalem to investigate. As the trial dragged on, Emperor Andronicus III died in 1341 and a civil war broke out in Byzantium between John Cantacuzenus and John V Palaeologus. Lazarus involved himself in these events on the side of Cantacuzenus, and in May 1346, he crowned him emperor. After that, Patriarch of Constantinople John Kalekas, a supporter of Palaeologus, deposed Lazarus and installed in his place Gerasimus, who departed to Jerusalem. With the triumph of Cantacuzenus in February 1347, the Byzantine government sent an embassy to the Egyptian sultan Nasir al-Din Hasan requesting Lazarus's reinstatement on the See of Jerusalem. Gerasimus arrived in Cairo in the fall of 1439, hoping to win the Mamluk authorities over to his side, but he died suddenly and so the question of Lazarus's return resolved itself.

During the persecution of Christians in the Mamluk state in 1354, Patriarch Lazarus was taken to Cairo, where he was thrown into prison and subject to beatings. He was arrested once again after the attack on Alexandria by the king of Cyprus in October 1365. By the autumn of 1366 the persecution ceased, partially thanks to the diplomatic intervention of the Byzantine emperor John V Palaeologus. Lazarus was allowed to go to Constantinople as part of a Mamluk embassy. The signatures of the patriarch of Jerusalem are found on several synodal acts of the Church of Constantinople from 1367 to 1368.[254]

In Lazarus's entourage in the mid-1360s was the Greek adventurer Paul Tagaris, who entered into the patriarch's trust to such a degree that he was appointed locum tenens of the See of Jerusalem during Lazarus's absence in Constantinople, and he later laid his claim for the patriarchate.[255]

Patriarch Dorotheus, who headed the Church of Jerusalem for nearly four decades in the late fourteenth and early fifteenth centuries, exemplifies the dual identity of the Middle Eastern Melkites. Several Greek manuscripts copied by the patriarch survive with Greek colophons, one of which is duplicated in Arabic. After Dorotheus, the patriarchate was inherited by his son Theophilus (before 1419–c. 1424), which indicated the existence of clerical dynasties in the Palestinian Melkite milieu, such as those that existed among the Nestorians, the Maronites, and the Antiochian Orthodox.[256] An Arabic colophon by a certain Jirjis al-Qudsi (i.e., "the Jerusalemite") referred to himself as the nephew of Patriarch Theophilus, which gives reason to believe that

Dorotheus and Theophilus were Arabs, albeit deeply integrated into Greek culture.[257]

The Russian pilgrim Zosima, who conversed with Theophilius in 1421, noted that "the priest Akim," who was in the patriarch's entourage, "has a command of both Arabic and Greek, is most beloved by the patriarch, [and] he wants to be one after him."[258] It seems that the dream of the "priest Akim" came true: apparently this is Patriarch Joachim who headed the Church of Jerusalem in the years 1426–1463.[259] There also survives an Arabic-language colophon by Joachim,[260] suggesting that the patriarch was of an Arab background.

In the entourage of the primate of Jerusalem, there were many Greeks as well as Arabs who left their names in manuscript marginalia from the thirteenth to the fifteenth centuries.[261] In general, bilingualism and even trilingualism was a common phenomenon among Middle Eastern clergy. More than fifty Greco-Arabic and four Greco-Syriac manuscripts survived from the Mamluk period, and the number of Arabic notes in Greek manuscripts can hardly be counted.[262] Taking into account the characteristic linguistic and cultural pride of the Byzantines, it is appropriate to assume that the majority of bilingual Melkites were Arabs, not Greeks.

In the neighboring Patriarchate of Antioch, Greek influence was not so clearly apparent. For several decades after Baybars's sacking of Antioch, the patriarchs of the city changed their residence and political orientation many times. The patriarchate's territory was divided among rival states—the Mamluk Sultanate, the possessions of the Crusaders, and Cilician Armenia. Byzantium continued to exert a strong influence on the Middle East. Different political patrons (Byzantium, Armenia, the Crusaders) put in place successive first hierarchs of Antioch, and from time to time, schisms occurred on this basis when conflicting candidates for the see were put forward in various parts of the patriarchate.

An Arabocentric perspective on the history of Middle Eastern Melkites has prevented researchers from discerning the role played by Cilician Armenia in the life of the Church of Antioch. But it was, essentially, a mini-Byzantium, with a compact Christian population, numerous Orthodox dioceses, and a Chalcedonian Armenian martial nobility that constituted a significant proportion (almost a quarter) of the ruling class.[263] It is no surprise that the local Orthodox episcopate repeatedly put forward from its own ranks candidates for patriarch of Antioch who often came into conflict with the protégés of other regional groups. At the same time, the Cilician patriarchs of Antioch, just like the Melkites of Syria and Palestine, viewed Constantinople as the center of the Christian world and sought recognition from the emperor and the patriarchs of Constantinople. The collapse of the Armenian kingdom in 1375, however, put an end to the Cilician power center within the patriarchate.

Euthymius I (before 1258–1277) was admitted into Antioch by Prince Bohemond and then driven out several times. Over the years, the patriarch enjoyed the hospitality of Michael VIII in Constantinople and the Hülegüid Abaqa Khan in Tabriz. After the fall of Antioch, he stayed in Cilicia, one of the few areas of his patriarchate that remained under Christian rule. There, Euthymius was involved in a conspiracy of Orthodox nobility against King Levon of Cilicia, and as a result, was thrown into prison in 1275, although he managed to escape to Constantinople. The patriarch remained in the Byzantine capital until his death. Severely ill, he summoned several Antiochian bishops to Constantinople to elect his successor. Michael Palaeologus, however, preferred for the see a Constantinopolitan monk of Frankish noble background, Theodosius de Villehardouin, who seemed more appropriate for his ecclesiastical policy of rapprochement with the West.[264]

After the Union of Lyon was rejected in Byzantium in 1282, Theodosius moved to the Crusaders' Syrian territory. He was succeeded in 1283–1284 by Arsenius, who previously was the bishop of Tripoli. After the death of Arsenius around 1286, on June 29, 1287, the bishops of the Syrian cities belonging to the Crusaders elected Cyril, the bishop of Tyre, as patriarch without the consent of the other bishops of the patriarchate. In turn, the bishops of Cilician Armenia proclaimed Dionysius, bishop of Cilician Pompeiopolis, to be patriarch, but Dionysius soon gave up the fight. Cyril arrived in Constantinople in the autumn of 1288, but for many years, he could not obtain official recognition from the Byzantine authorities, as for them he was associated with the Latin Crusaders. He was added to the diptychs of the Church of Constantinople only in 1296. Some authors attribute this change of attitude toward Cyril to the marriage of Emperor Michael IX and Princess Maria of Cilician Armenia. Recognizing Cyril was a friendly gesture by Constantinople toward the Cilician and other Antiochian bishops. If this conclusion holds true, then it would follow that the bishops of Cilicia, including Dionysius, were loyal to Cyril. In such case, it is a misconception on the part of Joseph Nasrallah to call Dionysius an "antipatriarch" during the years from 1287 to 1308.[265] The fall of the last Crusader states in Syria appears to have further strengthened the position of the Cilician bishops of the patriarchate. After the death of Cyril around 1308, Dionysius renewed his claims to the patriarchate. This time he was recognized by the Byzantine emperor and the ecumenical patriarch. Sometime after 1310, Dionysisus also moved to Constantinople, where he died in 1316.[266]

Patriarch Dionysius II, previously bishop of Mopsuestia, similarly to Dionysius I, was the protégé of the bishops of Cilician Armenia, where he resided during his patriarchate (late 1310s–1322). Before his death, he chose Sophronius, bishop of Tyre, to be his successor. Sophronius was recognized as patriarch in Cilicia; however, the bishops of southern Syria, taking advantage of the weakened ties with Cilician Armenia, elected as their own patriarch the metropolitan of Damascus, Abu al-Najm al-Arshi, and until his death, the Church of Antioch was in a state of schism.[267]

Byzantine influence once again became prominent from the 1340s to the 1370s, during the era of the debates over hesychasm. In 1344 Ignatius, an Armenian by origin—probably of a Chalcedonian Armenian background—was elected patriarch of Antioch. He arrived in Constantinople to receive approval and became involved in the ideological and political struggle around hesychasm and the teaching of Gregory Palamas.[268] Ignatius sided with Patriarch of Constantinople John Kalekas, an opponent of the Palamites. The Hodegon Monastery in Constantinople, where Ignatius and

his associate Metropolitan Arsenius of Tyre stayed, became
a center of anti-Palamite polemics. Around the end of 1345
or early 1346, Ignatius returned to the East, leaving Arsenius
as his representative in Constantinople. With the victory of
John Cantacuzenus in the internal conflict within Byzantium in 1347, the position of hesychasm within the empire
was greatly strengthened. The church council of 1351 definitively condemned the anti-Palamite views. Arsenius of Tyre
attempted to challenge the council's decisions before the
emperor, but then he left Constantinople. Patriarch Ignatius
at first accepted the decisions of the council but later, apparently under the influence of Arsenius, he once again took an
anti-Palamite position.

In the second half of the 1350s, Ignatius was deposed by
part of the clergy of Antioch who were oriented toward Constantinople and the Palamites. Pachomius, the metropolitan
of Damascus, was proclaimed the new patriarch. Ignatius
moved to Cyprus, under the protection of the ruling Lusignan dynasty. On Cyprus, there was a significant community
of Melkites from the Syro-Palestinian region. There, under
the auspices of the Latin authorities, a circle of Byzantine
intellectuals was formed with a pro-Catholic, anti-Palamite
orientation. The correspondence of Patriarch Callistus of
Constantinople with the Antiochian clergy in the years from
1360 to 1361 indicates that in Byzantium, Pachomius, a supporter of the hesychasts, was considered to be the legitimate
patriarch of Antioch. Starting with Pachomius, the residence
of the patriarchates of Antioch came to be in Damascus.[269]

An extensive correspondence survives between Patriarch
Philotheos Kokkinos of Constantinople (second patriarchate

in 1365–1376) with the clergy of Antioch. They discussed a wide range of issues, from attitudes toward hesychasm and the project of reconciliation with the Catholic Church to the canonical offenses of the abbot of Hodegon Monastery, the Antiochian metochion in the capital.[270] After the Mamluk persecution of 1365–1366, which financially ruined the Orthodox Church in the Middle East, Eastern bishops for the first time went to Russia seeking alms. Russian sources mention the arrival in 1371 of a Metropolitan Germanus from Egypt or Palestine, and in 1375–1376, Archimandrite Niphon from the Monastery of the Archangel in Jerusalem and a Metropolitan Mark, who was erroneously associated by them with the Monastery of Sinai. In fact, Mark seems to have come from the Patriarchate of Antioch. It is very likely that he can be identified with Patriarch Mark of Antioch (1376–1378).[271]

Nevertheless, this entire system of relations—the exchange of letters and embassies, visits by the Eastern patriarchs to Constantinople, and their participation in Byzantine church politics—collapsed in the early 1370s. From that time, not a single primate of the Middle Eastern churches paid a visit to the Byzantine capital. Correspondence with Constantinople was conducted periodically, but so little evidence of it remains that the weakening of ties is visible to the naked eye.

One might connect all these changes to the renewal and tightening of the Mamluk authorities' restrictions on the external contacts of the hierarchs of the Orthodox East after the Alexandrian Crusade. A very interesting source in this regard is the encyclopedic corpus of the Egyptian author al-Qalqashandi (d. 1418), which provides samples of letters issued by the Mamluk authorities to the heads of other religions confirming their authority, rights, and responsibilities. In them there are direct prohibitions on the patriarchs' maintaining unauthorized external relations, conducting correspondence with foreign rulers, or receiving messages from them, let alone traveling abroad.[272]

It is doubtful, however, that the increasing isolation of the Christian East could be connected to the Mamluk bans on the patriarchs' external contacts. It was hardly realistic to impose such a ban in a preindustrial society where there were no mechanisms for total control over people and ideas. The closing off of ties between Middle Eastern Christians and their coreligionists across the sea should be associated with a sort of internal crisis that led to the decline of the Orthodox cultures of the Eastern Mediterranean in the later Middle Ages.

The Church of Alexandria occupied a marginal position in the Orthodox East and rarely figures in the sources. Nevertheless, there are sufficient grounds to speak of its mixed Greek–Arabic character and to speculate that its relationship with the Greek world was closer than that of Jerusalem or Damascus.

Because of the small number of Alexandrian clergy, most patriarchs for that see were chosen from among the monks of Sinai, which was another channel of Greek influence. Sometimes, Byzantine church officials purposely sought to bring the liturgical practices and church traditions of the East closer to Greek models. Thus, the greatest Byzantine canonist of the turn of the twelfth to the thirteenth century,

Theodore Balsamon, who during the years 1185–1203 nominally occupied the See of Antioch, not only implemented this harmonization in his own Antiochian church but also sought to influence Patriarch Mark II of Alexandria. Mark, who was consecrated in Constantinople, upon arrival in Egypt discovered many customs and rituals common among the Egyptian Melkites that were unusual to him, and so he turned to Balsamon with a number of queries about the permissibility of such traditions.[273]

The Alexandrian primate, Nicholas II, was elected in 1263 under an agreement between Sultan Baybars and Emperor Michael Palaeologus to fill the See of Alexandria. Soon, however, the patriarch was in Byzantium, where he supported Patriarch Arsenius of Constantinople in his conflict with Michael Palaeologus, motivated by his attitude toward the Union of Lyon. Nicholas's successor Athanasius II (1276–1308/1315), who was elected to the patriarchate from the ranks of the monks of Sinai, also quickly moved to Constantinople, where he lived for more than thirty years. This patriarch was even more involved in the political and ideological confrontation between supporters and opponents of the union; however, with rare skill, he was able to hold an intermediate position on the issue so as to not be persecuted in the event of changes in the political situation. The patriarch's wily resourcefulness allowed him to remain "afloat" for decades, wrote Alexei Lebedev, "the patriarch continued to live in the capital without the troubles that overwhelmed overt supporters and opponents of union."[274]

Athanasius, who was fully absorbed with Byzantine church politics and forgot about his Egyptian flock, is rather

an exception among the patriarchs of Alexandria. His suc-
cessors, as a rule, lived in Egypt and some of them were even
Arabs or surrounded themselves with Arab clergy.[275] Thus,
Patriarch Gregory II (1315?–before 1335), also a former
Sinaite, translated the Typicon of Mar Saba into Arabic.[276]
On the territory of Egypt several church manuscripts from
the fourteenth and fifteenth centuries were produced,
both in Greek and in Arabic.[277] The last Arab patriarch of
Alexandria was Gregory V, born in Bostra. In a note in a
manuscript on Sinai, his disciple Joachim al-Karaki reports
Gregory's death in 1503, after twenty-three years of rule.[278]
This, however, is contrary to the dating established in the
scholarship for Patriarch Gregory's successor, Joachim I,
which is counted from 1486 to 1487.

The Athenian Joachim Pany ("The Glorious") is a truly
epic figure. This man is believed to have lived 116 years and
for almost 80 of them led the Church of Alexandria. Even
during his own lifetime, legends were told about him and
miracles attributed to him. The most famous of these legends recount that the ruler of Egypt, who can be identified
with the Mamluk sultan, Nasir Muhammad (1496–1498), at
the instigation of his Jewish advisors planned to exterminate
the Christians under his rule. Joachim was invited to debate
with the Jews in the presence of the sultan. The patriarch
was ordered to prove the truth of his faith by working a miracle: moving a mountain. The patriarch, along with all the
Christians, prayed and fasted for three days. The Theotokos
appeared to him in a dream and pointed him to a righteous
man, a one-eyed shoemaker, whose prayer would be heard

in heaven. On the appointed day, the patriarch together with the shoemaker commanded the mountain to move, and it split into three parts. Then the Jewish sage suggested a new test to Joachim: the patriarch had to drink a cup of poison to confirm the words of the Gospel that those with faith can drink deadly poison without harm. The patriarch managed to make the sign of the cross imperceptibly over the cup and drank the poison, which miraculously went out from him from below his ribs. Rinsing the bowl out with water, the patriarch then gave it to the Jewish scribe to drink, who then died a horrible death. The sultan, convinced of Joachim's holiness, gave the Christians all sorts of benefits and favors. He then supposedly converted to Christianity and ended his days in the Sinai Desert.[279]

The legend of the one-eyed shoemaker moving the mountain is a wandering literary topos; it originates in a legend about a similar miracle performed by the tenth-century Coptic patriarch Abraham ibn Zurʿa.[280] The theme of a Christian bishop harmlessly drinking poison is also found in the literature from the sixth century. Nevertheless, the legend of the miracle performed by Joachim is naturally interspersed with real information reflecting the competition between Christians and Jews to influence the Mamluk authorities in the late fifteenth and early sixteenth centuries, as well as, possibly, an attempted poisoning of the patriarch.

The Shadow of the West

In the first half of the fifteenth century, the Melkites of Syria and Palestine were involved in the attempt to unite the churches, culminating in the Council of Florence in 1439. Middle Eastern bishops did not demonstrate their own initiative in this matter and did not attend the council, instead delegating their powers to members of the Byzantine clergy. The representative of Patriarch Dorotheus of Antioch was Isidore, Metropolitan of Kiev; that of Patriarch Joachim of Jerusalem, Metropolitan Dorotheus of Monembasia; and that of Philotheus of Alexandria, Metropolitan Antonius of Heraclium.[281]

The decisions of the Council of Florence provoked an outcry in Byzantine society, as well as among the Orthodox of the Middle East. In April 1443, on the initiative of Metropolitan Arsenius of Caesarea in Cappadocia who had arrived in the Holy City, the three Eastern patriarchs gathered in Jerusalem and denounced the union and its advocate, Patriarch Metrophanes of Constantinople. The correspondence of Patriarch of Constantinople Gennadius Scholarius with the monks of Sinai in the mid-1450s also indicates the strong anti-Latin sentiment among Middle Eastern monastics.[282]

At the same time, after the fall of Constantinople and the destruction of other Orthodox states of the Balkan and Black Sea region, the Middle Eastern patriarchs were faced with the need to find new political and financial backers. In August 1456, the papal legate Moïse Giblet was sent to the Middle East with the aim of strengthening Rome's position in the region on the eve of a planned crusade by European sovereigns against the Ottomans. Giblet held talks on cooperation with the emir of the Gharb region in Southern Lebanon and met with Patriarch Michael III of Antioch, whom he invited to renew a union with Rome. From Syria, the legate went to Egypt, where he discussed similar issues with Patriarch Mark of Alexandria, and then settled in Cyprus, from which he conducted a correspondence with the Eastern patriarchs. Coming to the throne of Antioch at the end of 1456, Patriarch Mark III yielded to Giblet's urgings and in February 1457 established a commemoration of the pope in the Church of Antioch and began corresponding with Rome. Mark III died around late 1457 or early 1458, and then Joachim III, former bishop of Hama and a longtime supporter of the union, became Patriarch of Antioch. In June 1458, he arrived in Palestine and met with Patriarch Joachim of Jerusalem and Patriarch Mark of Alexandria in the village of Rama or Ramallah. The patriarch of Jerusalem succumbed to the persistent entreaties of his colleagues and joined the union.[283]

Shortly thereafter, in November 1458, the dome of the Church of the Resurrection cracked during an earthquake.

At considerable cost, Joachim secured permission from the authorities to restore the dome. However, as the work was nearing completion, Muslim jurists decided to revise their decision and ordered that the restored areas be destroyed. The costs of litigation and the expenses of reconstruction fully depleted the patriarch of Jerusalem's coffers.[284] Obviously hoping for financial support from the Catholic West, in May and June 1459, Joachim signed a letter of the Eastern patriarchs urging the princes of Europe to undertake a crusade, as well as sending a message on his own behalf to the pope.

Having received authority as the representative of the Eastern patriarchs and the emir of Gharb, Moïse Giblet sailed to Italy and on April 21, 1460, signed a pact of union with Rome on behalf of the Eastern patriarchs. In commemoration of this event, the pope ordered translated into Latin the patriarchs' Arabic documents related to their acceptance of the union. These texts were merged into the codex Liber Rubeus, which was preserved in the Vatican archives.

Already by the seventeenth century, scholars were questioning the authenticity of the contents of the Liber Rubeus. Indeed, false emissaries purporting to be from various Eastern rulers are known to have arrived in Rome in the second half of the fifteenth century with offers of a military alliance against the Turks and even ecclesiastical union. These missions were organized by adventurers from within the papal entourage for propaganda purposes or their own benefit. Arabic sources do not confirm the existence in the 1450s of patriarchs Mark and Joachim of Antioch. The debate about the authenticity of Giblet's embassy and the union of 1458 has continued into modern times and is far from having been resolved.[285]

However, even if we consider the union of the three patriarchs with Rome to have actually taken place, it is clear that the patriarchs, especially Joachim of Jerusalem, soon realized the futility of hoping for aid from the Catholic world. Joachim realized that he needed to look for patrons elsewhere and appealed to the grand prince of Moscow for support. The patriarch personally left to seek alms in Russia, but along the way, in Caffa, he fell ill and died in late 1463 or early 1464. Before his death, he sent a message to Moscow describing the adversity facing the Church of Jerusalem and requesting help. The letter was delivered by his nephew Joseph who, in accordance with the late patriarch's will, was consecrated metropolitan of Caesarea Philippi by the metropolitan of Moscow and was sent home with lavish gifts. The event of a journey to Russia by the patriarch of Jerusalem was extensively utilized by the Muscovite ecclesiastical hierarchy and scribes, and it became one of the elements shaping the concept of Russian messianism.[286]

Middle Eastern churches, however, remained willing to accept alms from any benefactor. The monks of the Monastery of Sinai, who were revered far beyond the Orthodox world, were the most broad-minded. According to some accounts, the monastery had chapels for the Syrian Jacobites, the Armenians, and the Copts. The Monastery of Sinai received lavish alms from aristocrats and rulers of European countries. Thus, in the late fifteenth century, the monastery was granted annual subsidies from King Louis XI of France, Queen Isabella of Spain, and Emperor Maximilian I. Considerable sums were donated by pilgrims. In the fifteenth century, the monastery designated a special cell and, later,

a chapel dedicated to St Catherine, to be used by pilgrims
for Latin-rite services. Such friendly relations between the
Monastery of Sinai and Catholic Europe were a unique phenomenon in the late medieval world. At the same time, in
terms of dogma and ritual, the monks of Sinai remained in
the bosom of Orthodox tradition, something emphasized
by all Western observers. It is known in particular that the
Sinaites sought the views of Patriarch of Constantinople
Gennadius Scholarius (1454–1456) as to whether it was per-
missible to offer prayers for the king of Bosnia who sent the
monastery gifts but held a pro-Catholic orientation.[287]

The Flemish chronicler of the late fifteenth century,
Theodoric Pauli wrote that Duke Philip of Burgundy provided annual assistance to the Church of Jerusalem and renovated the Church of the Holy Sepulchre with the sultan's
consent.[288] Once again, however, this assistance did not affect
the doctrinal views of the patriarchs of Jerusalem.

In 1484, Patriarch Symeon of Constantinople held a
church council at which the Orthodox Church definitively
rejected the Union of Florence and approved a rite of recep-
tion of Catholics into Orthodoxy, designed to maximally
facilitate the return of Greeks living in territories conquered
by the Ottomans from the Latins, to the faith of their fathers.
Although some copies of the council's acts refer to the participation of all the Middle Eastern patriarchs in the work
of the council, this assertion seems implausible. It is more
correct to assume that the sees of Alexandria and Jerusalem
were represented by exarchs from among the bishops of the
Church of Constantinople.[289]

Epilogue

Our understanding of the dynamics of the development of the Middle Eastern Orthodox community under the Mamluks is extremely scanty. However, through the fragmentary data provided by the sources, a picture emerges of an acutely deepening crisis in Middle Eastern Christianity at the turn of the fifteenth to the sixteenth century.

Under pressure from the Bedouins, the Christian population left Shawbak.[290] The Christian quarter of Hebron disappeared.[291] Monasteries died out, including the Monastery of St John the Evangelist by the Jordan, which was turned into a lair of Bedouin bandits. In the late fourteenth and early fifteenth centuries, pilgrims counted between fifteen and thirty monks at the Monastery of Mar Saba, but by the end of the fifteenth century, something on the order of five or six remained and at the turn of the fifteenth to the sixteenth century, the Lavra had been abandoned by the monks for some time under onslaught from the Bedouins.[292] Pilgrims visiting Sinai in the fourteenth century spoke of hundreds of inhabitants in the Monastery of St Catherine (the most modest figures are between 200 and 240 people), whereas in the first half of the fifteenth century, there were only fifty to sixty and in the second half of the same century, only thirty to fifty. Finally, the traveler Arnold von Harff found only eight people there in 1497. After 1478, any mention of bishops of Sinai disappears for sixty years.[293]

The sultan Qansuh al-Ghawri, ruling at the sunset of the Mamluk era, was indifferent to religious matters, but public opinion in Egypt was hostile to non-Muslim minorities, who faced severe discrimination. This situation was exacerbated by the state's financial problems, which authorities tried to resolve partially through an extraordinary taxation of *dhimmis*. Portuguese expansion in the Indian Ocean, which undermined Egypt's foreign trade, caused a hardening of attitudes toward Christians, especially those from the West. In a letter to the pope of Rome in 1503, the Mamluk sultan threatened to destroy the Christian holy places of Palestine and Sinai. The Church of the Holy Sepulchre was closed during the years 1511–1512.

Fifteen letters sent by Qansuh al-Ghawri to the Monastery of St Catherine on Mount Sinai have been preserved. Most of these decrees formally confirm the monastery's traditional privileges: the duty-free delivery of goods through Egyptian ports, the free passage of pilgrims and the monastery's alms collectors, and the inviolability of the monastery's endowment properties in various parts of the sultanate. From these documents, however, it can be seen that in times of crisis in the Mamluk state, the authorities were unable to protect from attack remote metochia or even the monastery itself, which was captured and sacked by Bedouins around 1505. The abbot attempted to persuade the Bedouins to return stolen property, but they killed him and, so far as we can determine, the authorities failed to punish those responsible.[294]

The reasons for this decline of the Orthodox East are not entirely clear. A number of explanations could be put forward, from the general environmental crisis in the region of Syria and Palestine to the establishment of Portuguese hegemony over the South Seas. Naturally, not only did the crisis affect the Orthodox but also, by the end of the fifteenth century, only one monk was left in each of the enormous Coptic monasteries, and Nestorian monasteries had disappeared completely. In the last third of the fifteenth and beginning of the sixteenth centuries, the Mamluk state experienced a severe decline and clearly was losing in the conflict with its nomadic periphery.

Another important factor is that around the turn of the century, there was a certain disorganization in the ecclesiastical and social structures of the Arab–Christian world and its acute weakening. As a result, the ecclesio-political vacuum was filled by immigrants from the more viable Orthodox communities of the Balkans. At the turn of the fifteenth to the sixteenth century, with amazing synchronicity, the Greeks gained control of the Patriarchate of Alexandria and of the Monastery of Sinai, and later, the Church of Jerusalem.

The blows suffered by the Middle Eastern Orthodox churches during the first nine hundred years of Muslim rule led to a significant reduction in their flocks, their territory, and the number of their dioceses.

This waning of ecclesiastical structures affected the Patriarchate of Alexandria most of all. For the entire period from the seventh through the fifteenth centuries, we know the names of a few more than a dozen diocesan bishops. The sources from the ninth through the thirteenth centuries mention around six sees. The number of dioceses constantly decreased: in the ninth century, there were about three; in the fourteenth century, no more than two; and by the fifteenth century, all but one had disappeared apart from the patriarchal see. The consecration of the patriarch of Alexandria came to be performed by neighboring Eastern patriarchs outside Egypt. The Orthodox population in Egypt was small and continued to decline. From around three hundred thousand people at the time of the Arab conquest of Egypt (around 5 percent of the total population of Egyptian Christians), the Melkite community decreased to around ninety thousand by the beginning of the thirteenth century and to just a few thousand in the Ottoman period.[295]

Toward the end of the sixth century, the Patriarchate of Antioch consisted of 151 episcopal sees, including seventeen metropolitans. For the tenth and eleventh centuries, we know the names of the bishops for about a dozen sees. There is relatively complete information on the number of dioceses in the Church of Antioch starting from the fourteenth and fifteenth centuries. Their number does not exceed fifteen to twenty. Many ancient archdioceses had entirely disappeared, including Hieropolis (Manbij), Anazarbus, Seleucia Isauria, Sergiopolis, Dara, and Samosata.[296] In Byzantine times, there were around sixty sees in the Patriarchate of Jerusalem, whereas at the beginning of the Ottoman era there were no more than three. Many cities that previously had been diocesan centers simply ceased to exist, especially those along the Mediterranean coast, which had been ravaged by the wars between the Mamluks and the Crusaders, and

Transjordan, which was most effected by the consequences of the ecological crisis and desertification. In many other areas where urban life still flickered, the Christian population disappeared.

Thus, to sum up the first nine centuries of the life of the Christian East under Muslim rule, it should be noted that the flourishing of Middle Eastern Christians in the first century AH was replaced by a progressive crisis, a worsening in the social situation of Christians, a reduction in their numbers, and cultural decline. These processes reached their peak in the Mamluk Sultanate, which came to be replaced by a new type of state, the Ottoman Empire, to which the fate of Middle Eastern Christians became inextricably bound for the next four centuries, during which the Christian East experienced an unexpected demographic and cultural revival.

Timeline

622   Hijra—When Muhammad and his followers migrated from Mecca for Yathrib (Medina), marking the start of the Islamic calendar

634   Battle of Ajnadayn in Palestine. The first major defeat of a Byzantine army by Muslim Arab invaders. Damascus falls to the Muslim armies soon thereafter

636   Battle of Yarmouk. An even more decisive Byzantine defeat followed shortly after by the fall of Jerusalem to the Muslim armies

637   Patriarch Sophronius of Jerusalem dies and see left vacant

641   The Islamic conquest of Egypt begins

661   Beginning of Ummayad Caliphate centered in Damascus

679   The Ummayad Caliph Muʿawiya restores the church in Edessa, previously damaged by earthquake

681   Sixth Ecumenical Council in Constantinople condemns Monothelitism

717   Founding of Ramla as the new capital of Palestine

720s   Coptic Christians begin frequent rebellions against higher taxation following on from the land survey of 697 AD

c. 730 While serving as a tax official of the Muslim Caliph St John of Damascus writes his treatise on the Holy Icons

740s   First translations of Christian literature into Arabic from Greek and Syriac

787   Seventh Ecumenical Council in Constantinople restores the veneration of icons and includes the epistle of Patriarch Theodore of Jerusalem to the patriarchs of Alexandria and Antioch upholding this teaching

1014 The caliph allowed *dhimmis* to migrate out of Egypt and a mass exodus of Christians to Byzantine territory began. Many of those who remain convert to Islam

1031 The Byzantines recapture Edessa. Half of the territory of the Antiochian Patriarchate is again part of the Byzantine Empire

1071 The Byzantine army is defeated by the Seljuks Turks at Manzikert, leading to the Byzantine loss of control of most of Asia Minor

1098 The Western Crusaders begin to establish parallel Latin bishoprics

1099 Establishment of Latin Kingdom of Jerusalem

1187 Battle of Hattin. Salah al-Din destroys the Crusaders' army and seizes almost the entire territory of the Kingdom of Jerusalem

1217 Crusader invasion of Egypt begins leading to massacres of both local Muslims and Christians

1258 Mongol siege of Baghdad

1260 Mamluks defeat the Mongols at the battle of Ayn Jalut

1268 Mamluks capture Antioch and largely destroy the city

1324 Following another major earthquake the Patriarchate abandons Antioch and relocates to Damascus

1347– The Black Death pandemic is estimated to kill one-third of
1348 the population. Famine follows

1354 Sharia law restrictions again applied to Coptic Christians leading to renewed persecution

1371 Middle Eastern Orthodox clergy begin to travel to Russia seeking financial support

1443 The patriarchs of Alexandria, Antioch, and Jerusalem meet to denounce the false reunion with the Latin church announced at the Council of Florence in 1439

Notes

1 Late Antique civilization is approximately the late third to the early eighth century AD.

2 Monophysitism is the belief that Christ had only a single Divine nature. Acceptance of this belief led to schisms from the Church following the Council of Chalcedon in 451 AD.

3 The Monothelete dogma was the belief that Christ while possessing two natures, fully human and divine, had only a single Will.

4 For more on the Arab conquests and the reactions thereto by the people of the Near East, see Bol'shakov, vol. 2; see also Krivov, "Otnoshenie"; for excerpts from sources and essential commentaries, see Mednikov, vols. 1–2.

5 Melkites means "royal" (from the Syr. *malka* for "king"), a term used to denote Middle Eastern adherents of the doctrine of Chalcedon, that is, the faith of the Byzantine emperors. In contemporary scholarly literature, the term "Melkites" refers to the Arabic- and Syriac-speaking Orthodox Christians of the medieval Middle East, in this way distinguishing them from the Orthodox of Asia Minor and the Balkans, who belonged to the Greco-Byzantine cultural sphere. Later on, the Arab Uniate community took on this self-designation, having broken away from the Orthodox Patriarchate of Antioch. Therefore, as applied to medieval realities, the term "Melkites" means the Orthodox, and for the eighteenth and nineteenth centuries, it designates Arab Uniates of the Byzantine rite. In the present study, the term "Melkites" is used to mean "the Orthodox population of the

Middle East," if we are talking about the period before eighteenth century, when the Uniate Antiochian church emerged.

6 For an analysis of this document, see Mednikov, 1.556–99.

7 The "rightly guided caliphs" lived in the period of thirty years after the death of Muhammad and prior to the creation of the Umayyad Caliphate in 661 AD.

8 *Dhimmi* (Arabic: *ahl al-dhimma* "the protected people") is in Islamic law a term for nonbelievers who were subjects of the Islamic state. For more on the legal evolution of the status of *dhimmis*, see, for example, Mednikov, vol. 1.

9 Mednikov, 1.566–600; Bartol'd, "Review," 511; Bartol'd, "Islam i melkity," 651–652; Hitti, 422–424, 485–486; Atiya, 82, 84, 193, 198, 267–268; Runciman, *A History of the Crusades*, 1.20–23.

10 Under Islamic law, a Muslim man can marry a Christian woman; a Christian man, however, must convert to Islam in order to marry a Muslim woman.

11 Runciman, *A History of the Crusades*, 1.23–25; Fargues, 49–51.

12 Atiya, 82, 84, 193, 267, 68; Runciman, *A History of the Crusades*, 1.25–26; Mednikov, 1.649–650, 841–842; Bol'shakov, *Istoriia* 2.124–127; Bol'shakov, "Vizantiia i Khalifat"; Mets, 44–45, 54–55.

13 N. A. Ivanov, *Programa*, 5.

14 It may be, however, that this is something peculiar to the sources: almost nothing is known about the Jewish community under the Umayyad. Borrut and Donner, 3–5.

15 The territory of Egypt was divided into smaller administrative districts managed by governors from among the Christian Copts. This system was convenient for both farmers and the lower bureaucracy, allowing them to understate the actual volumes of agricultural

products and to withhold taxes on newly-plowed land. During the first half-century of Arab rule, Egypt prospered and was completely loyal. On the status of Upper Mesopotamia in the first decades of the Caliphate, see Robinson. On the situation of the Copts, see Brett, 6–7.

16 Piccirilo, 48, 53–54; Zeyadeh, 118ff.; MacAdam, 51; Shick, 86–87; Bisheh 78.

17 MacAdam, 57–59, 72–74, 76, 82; Zeyadeh, 121–124; Griffith, "'Abd al-Masih an-Nagrani," 357; Shick, 86–87.

18 The chapel erected over the Holy Sepulchre, the sacred center of the Church of the Resurrection in Jerusalem.

19 Arculf, 1–12; Willibald, 13–22; Bernard the Wise, 23–31.

20 MacAdam, 77–78, 81; *EAEHL*, 190, 270–285, 384, 927–930, 1035–1050.

21 Neale, 67–80; Eutychius, 46; Matveevskii, 229–233.

22 Murav'ev, *Istoriia*, 1.286, 299–305; Kulakovskii, 197–198; Potulov, 40–41.

23 Eutychius, 13, 27; Mednikov, *Istoriia*, 2.260–261, 271; Potulov, 40; Karalevskij, "Antioche," col. 595.

24 Palmer, 30.

25 Whitcomb, 11–28.

26 Borrut and Donner, 1–3. On Mu'awiya's religious policy, see also Humphreys, 85–114.

27 Bol'shakov, *Istoriia*, 1.115, 176; Mednikov, 1.651.

28 Eutychius, 38; (Russian translation: Mednikov, 2(1).272); Bartold, "Review," 582.

29 Kekelidze, 144.

30 Bartol'd, "Islam i melkity," 652; see also Panchenko, "Rod Ioanna Damaskina," 88–99.

31 Bartol'd, "Islam i melkity," 653.

32 Potulov, 45; Todt, "Notitia," 173; Moosa, 101–104; Karalevskij, "Antioche," col. 591–592.

33 Moosa, 114–116.

34 *SCWSC*, 202–204; Mednikov, 2(1).273, 1.683–686.

35 Eutychius, 41 (Russian translation: Mednikov, 2.273).

36 Neale, 80, 86; Matveevskii, 233–235.

37 Sasanian coinage was the currency of the Persian/Iranian *Sasanian* Empire (224–651).

38 Mednikov, 2.89–90; Bol'shakov, *Istoriia*, 3.274–282; Bol'shakov, "Vizantiia i khalifat," 357.

39 Eutychius, 42; For a discussion of this issue, see Mednikov, 1.687–699.

40 Mednikov, 1.701.

41 Eutychius, 43–44 (Russian translation: Mednikov, 2. 275–276); Mednikov, 1.704–722; Bol'shakov, *Istoriia* 4.139–147; for contemporary polemics around the religious politics of 'Umar, see Levi-Rubin and Yarbrough.

42 Theophanes, year 6215.

43 Kekelidze, 151–157; Griffith, "The Mansur Family."

44 Leo III the Isaurian (717–743): Byzantine emperor and initiator of the iconoclast policy.

45 Theophanes, year 6255.

46 Murav'ev, *Istoriia* 1.319–322, 330, 334–337.

47 Eutychius, 45 (Russian translation: Mednikov, 2.276–277); Mednikov, 1.723; Bartol'd, "Islam i melkity," 653–654; Theophanes, year 6234.

48 Kekelidze, 166; Eutychius, 52; Mednikov, 2.278, 285, 287, 288, 290, 329–330; Todt, "Notitia," 184–185.

49 Theophanes, year 6234.

50 Ibid., year 6248.

51 Mednikov, 1.775, 2.285; Bartol'd, "Islam i melkity," 654; Todt, "Notitia," 178–179.

52 Griffith, "The Mansur Family."

53 Brooks; K. A. Panchenko, "K istorii pravoslavnogo letopisaniia."

54 Wright, 111; Papadopulo-Keramevs, i–iii.

55 Loparev, "Vizantiiskie zhitie sviatykh," 76ff.; *Zhitie Romana Novogo*; Papadopulo-Keramevs, *Muchenichestvo shestidesiati novykh sviatykh muchenikov*.

56 Theophanes, year 6234; *Zhitie Petra Kapetoliiskogo*.

57 *Zhitie Antoniia/Ravakha*; "Istoricheskoe skazanie o podvizhnichestve Ilii Novogo"; Loparev, "Vizantiiskie zhitiia sviatykh," XIX.45; "Skazanie o muchenichestve sviatykh ottsov v lavre prep. Savvy," 47.

58 Griffith, "'Abd al-Masih an-Nagrani," 333–335, 351–359.

59 Uspenskii, *Pervoe puteshestvie*, 108–119.

60 Willibald, 19.

61 Loparev, *Vizantiiskie zhitiia* sviatykh, 19.28.

62 Ibid., 24.

63 Brett, 6–7.

64 Neale, 1.114–118; Mednikov, 1.736–737.

65 Browne, 57–58; Runciman, *A History of the Crusades*, 1.26–27.

66 Theophanes, year 6267. Theophanes clearly borrows this passage from the Syriac Melkite chronicle of 780.

67 Theophanes, year 6272; Mednikov, 1.744–747; 755–757; 759–760.

68 Mednikov, 1.720–722, 724, 736, 744–745, 748, 757, 768.

69 Burns, 111–112.

70 Zeyadeh, 120; MacAdam, 57, 74–81.

71 Piccirillo, 48; Shick, 87–88. Bisheh, 100–101.

72 Nasrallah, *Histoire*, 3(1).69.

73 Piccirillo, 47.

74 "Skazanie o muchenichestve sviatykh ottsov v lavre prep. Savvy."

75 "Skazanie o muchenichestve sviatykh ottsov v lavre prep. Savvy," 9.

76 Loparev, Vizantiiskie zhitiia sviatykh, 19.32.

77 Finkelstein, 60, 61, 64.

78 Theophanes, years 6301 and 6305.

79 Atiya, 86; Brett, 7, 15; Panchenko, *"Koptskii bunt."*

80 Brett, "Population," 15.

81 Piccirillo, 53–55.

82 Swanson, 63.

83 Treiger, "Miracles of St. Eustratius"; Treiger, "Paterikon."

84 Hiyari, 134.

85 Burns, 142, 144, 156.

86 Brett, "Population," 3, 8–10.

87 Brett, "Population," 18–19.

88 Ibid., 15.

89 Griffith, "The Monks of Palestine," 17–20.

90 Griffith, "Greek into Arabic," 122–123.

91 Ibid., 124–128.

92 For the bibliography on these figures, see Griffith, "The Monks of Palestine," 22–23; Boiko, 53–60; Panchenko, "K istorii pravoslavnogo letopisaniia," 109; Panchenko, "Kosta ibn Luka," 162.

93 Griffith, 6, 24.

94 Eutychius, 49.

95 Panchenko, "K istorii pravoslavnogo letopisaniia," 109–120; Panchenko, "Vospriiatie istoricheskogo protsessa," 82–86.

96 Eutychius, 75 (Russian translation: Mednikov, 2.288–289).

97 Eutychius, 55 (Russian translation: Mednikov, 2.280).

98 Griffith, "Greek into Arabic," 125; Griffith, "The Monks of Palestine," 15–17.

99 Lopaerev, *Vizantiiskie zhitiia sviatykh*, 19.23, 29–30; Mednikov, 2(1).288–289; Theophanes, year 6255.

100 V. V. Bartol'd, "Karl Velikii i Kharun al-Rashid"; V. V. Bartol'd, "K voprosu o franko-musul'manskikh otnosheniiakh."

101 Bernard the Wise, 26; Bartol'd, "Karl Velikii i Kharun al-Rashid," 293; Dmitrievskii, "Drevneishie patriarshie Tikikony," 63–64.

102 Loparev, "Vizantiiskie zhitiia sviatykh," 17.215; Bartol'd, "Karl Velikii i Kharun al-Rashid," 291.

103 Loparev, "Vizantiiskie zhitiia sviatykh," 17.215–216.

104 Griffith, "The Life of Theodore of Edessa," 152–156.

105 Neale, 82–96; Mednikov, 1.649–650, 683–687, 701–702.

106 "Skazanie o muchenichestve sviatykh ottsov v lavre prep. Savvy," 32–35.

107 Eutychius, 55–56; Mednikov, 1.762–764, 2.279–282.

108 Mednikov, 1.778–788; Hitti, 543–545; Fil'shtinskii, 133–142.

109 Mednikov, 1.791, 804, 805, 809–810, 813; 2.291–293, 330–331.

110 Panchenko, "Razrushenie damasskoi tserkvi"; Treiger A., "Unpublished Texts from the Arab Orthodox Tradition."

111 Mets, 16; Rozen, 89.

112 The Kabba is a small shrine situated near the center of the Great Mosque in Mecca, Islam's holiest city. Muslims orientate themselves toward this during the five ritual times of daily prayer and process around it during the annual pilgrimage to Mecca.

113 Rozen, 110–122; Mets, 17; Runciman, *A History of the Crusades*, 1.30–31; Bol'shakov, "Vizantiia i khalifat," 364–365.

114 N. A. Mednikov, 2.335–336.

115 N. A. Mednikov, 1.821–824, 2.335–336, 338–342, 343–346; K. A. Panchenko, "Antiokhiiskii patriarkh Khristofor," 223–227.

116 V. R. Rozen, 32–33, 40–41, 240–259, 309–331; N. A. Mednikov, 1.825–838; Runciman, *A History of the Crusades*, 1.31–34; Kuchuk-Ioannesov, "Pis'mo Tsimiskhiia," 96–100.

117 Eutychius, 88; N. A. Mednikov, 2.294.

118 Dmitrievskii, "Drevneishie patriarshie Tikikony," 36, 40, 49, 63.

119 Brett, "Al-Karaza al-Marqusiya," 36–37.

120 Mednikov, 1.840–841; Mets, 57.

121 Rozen, 35, 295–300; Mets, 58.

122 Mednikov, 1.840–841; Mets, 57; Sanders; Wilfong, 175–197; Lev, 179–196.

123 Rozen, 42–43, 337–338; Mednikov, 1.839–840, 849, 2.357–358; Moiseeva and Panchenko.

124 Mednikov, 1.849–853; Mets, 58–59.

125 Mednikov, 1.853–854, 2.360–371; Rozen, 48.

126 Yahya, 201; Rozen, 48, 49, 356–357.

127 Mednikov, 1.854–857; Mets, 59.

128 A significant figure in the history of the late Fatimid Caliphate is the vizier Badr al-Jamali, the *de facto* ruler of the state at the end of the eleventh century. A *ghulam* (slave-soldier) of Armenian ethnicity, thus hardly a sincere convert to Islam, he relied on the forces of Armenian mercenaries, many of whom were Christians. Badr treated Coptic patriarchs with marked respect. At the same time, the church was strictly subordinated to the interests of the state.

Christians and Jews had to pay *jizya* without exceptions. The vizier dictated resolutions to the council of Coptic bishops, making use of biblical terminology, in a manner similar to Christian emperors in the era of the ecumenical councils (Brett, "Al-Karaza al-Marqusiya," 50–52).

129 Bartol'd, "Review," 590–591; Bartol'd, "Islam i melkity," 655; Yahya, 237, 239; Mednikov, 1.857–860.

130 Bartol'd, "Review," 592; Bartol'd, "K voprosu o franko-musul'manskikh otnosheniiakh," 295; Yahya, 252; Mets, 46.

131 Michael the Syrian, 160–161; Matthew of Edessa, 84–85.

132 Rozen, 1–2, 4, 22, 86–87, 90.

133 The commander-in-chief of the guard units stationed in the eastern part of the empire.

134 Rozen, 3–11, 24–25, 33, 124–127, 209.

135 Arkim. Leonid, "Tri stati," 44–45.

136 Runciman, *Vostochnaia skhizma*, 54–56; Archim. Ledonid, "Tri stati," 45. On Byzantine rule in Antioch in the late tenth and eleventh centuries, see also Briun, 1.143–214.

137 Eutychius; Yahya.

138 See, in excerpt, Rozen, 36–48; Mets, 139–141; Krachkovskii, "Arabskaia geograficheskaia literatura," 266–267.

139 A Byzantine title of middle rank.

140 Zayat.

141 Kekelidze, 119–23.

142 Nasrallah, *Histoire*, 3 (1).191–229.

143 Marv is a city on the historical silk road in present-day Turkmenistan.

144 Bartol'd, "Islam i melkity," 655. [The Khwarezm is an ancient territory on the shores of the Aral Sea now divided between present-day Kazakhstan, Uzbekistan, and Turkmenistan.]

145 AH dating is the Islamic system. The abbreviation is derived from the Latin: Anno Hegirae, "in the year of the Hijra," or 622 AD, the year in which Muhammad and his followers migrated from Mecca to Yathrib (Medina).

146 Krivov, "Araby-khristiane," 250–255.

147 V Rozen, 45–47; see also Kuzenkov and Panchenko, 5–6.

148 Bartol'd, "Review," 585.

149 Nicephorus Bryennius, 105–108; F. I. Uspenskii, 3.40–43; Runciman, *A History of the Crusades* 1.64–72.

150 Runciman, *A History of the Crusades* 1.73–75; Michael the Syrian, Part 1, 30. Mikhail, 151–162.

151 Graf, 2.98–100; Nasrallah, *Histoire*, 3(1).86–89.

152 Bat Yeor, 2.48–49.

153 Runciman, *A History of the Crusades* 1.76–78; Nasrallah, *Histoire*, 3(1).103–104.

154 Runciman, *A History of the Crusades* 1.195–217, 235–250, 261–287; Runciman, *Vostochnaia skhizma*, 67–69; F. I. Uspenskii, 3.107–115.

155 Runciman, *A History of the Crusades*, 1.222, 252, 257, 277, 289; Runciman, *Vostochnaia skhizma*, 66, 68–69.

156 Runciman, *Vostochnaia skhizma*, 69.

157 Runciman, *A History of the Crusades*, 1.288–289; Runciman, *Vostochnaia skhizma*, 69.

158 Popov, 227–230; Plank, 188.

159 Jotischky, 91.

160 Plank, 187; Nasrallah, *Histoire*, 3(1).104–105.

161 Arkhim. Leontii, xxv–xxxvii; Plank, 187–188; Rose, 241; Belen'kaia, *Leontii II,* 527–531.

162 P. Plank, 186.

163 Runciman, *A History of the Crusades*, 1.320; Runciman, *Vostochnaia skhizma*, 69.

164 Runciman, *A History of the Crusades*, 1.257. Burns, however, argues that there was an Orthodox bishop in the city before the arrival of the Crusaders (Burns, *Monuments of Syria*, 57). In this case, the separation of the Orthodox and Catholic ecclesiastical institutions in the East should be counted from autumn of 1098.

165 F. I. Uspenskii, 3.116–120.

166 Runciman, *A History of the Crusades*, 1.305–306, 320–321; Runciman, *Vostochnaia skhizma*, 72; Briun, 2.19–31, 39–41.

167 J. Richard, 154–155; Jotischky, 91; P. Plank, 185.

168 P. Plank, 185; Jotischky, 91–92.

169 Jotischky, 85.

170 Daniil, 49, 55, 59, 61; Sæwulf, 286.

171 Daniil, 123; Runciman, *A History of the Crusades*, 1.294–295; Runciman, *Vostochnaia skhizma*, 69–70; Richard, 150–60; Pahlitzsch, "Georgians and Greeks," 35–39.

172 Jotischky, 93; Runciman, *Vostochnaia skhizma*, 70–71; Richard, 154–155.

173 John Phocas, 46–47, 50–52; Jotischky, 93.

174 Sharon, 50–52.

175 Pahlitzsch, 36.

176 Jotischky, 93.

177 John Phocas, 49; Jotischky, 90, 92; Frenkel, 111–112; Pahlitzsch, "Georgians and Greeks," 36–37.

178 Plank, 184; J. Richard, 151–157; Rose, 240–241.

179 Plank, 183–184.

180 Plank, 186; Griffith, "Anthony David of Bagdad," 19.

181 Runciman, *A History of the Crusades*, 1.320–321, 3.87–91, 99–100, 135–138, 231; Runciman, *Vostochnaia skhizma*, 71–75; F. I. Uspenskii, 3.149–155, 205–220; Karalevskij, "Antioche," col. 618–619; Briun, 2.97–150, 158–168, 178–184, 312–444.

182 Rose, 239–249; Pahlitzsch, "Georgians and Greeks," 37–39.

183 Matveevskii, 365–370; Runciman, *A History of the Crusades*, 3.150–169; Runciman, *Vostochnaia skhizma*, 76; Panchenko, "Nikolai I."

184 Rose, 241; Porphyry Uspenskii, *Vtoroe puteshestvie*, 246. Grumel proposes placing the death of Euthymius at 1230 ("La Chronologie des patriarches Grecs," 197–198).

185 Matveevskii, 367–369; Atiya, 92.

186 Ibn al-ʿAdim, 163.

187 Michael the Syrian, Part 3, 17–20.

188 Atiya, 94. (An ancient region of northeastern Africa straddling present-day Egypt and Sudan.)

189 Michael the Syrian, Part 5, 50.

190 Atiya, 95.

191 Atiya, 94–95; Matveevskii, 367–369.

192 Sava Nemanjić, 1–4, 17–21, 30–39; Pahlitzsch, "Georgians and Greeks," 39; Pahlitzsch, "Athanasios II," 465–474; Grumel, "La Chronologie des patriarches Grecs," 198–199.

193 The Chingizids were the descendants of Genghis Khan, the founder of the Mongol dynasty.

194 Runciman, *A History of the Crusades*, 3.306.

195 Ibid., 307.

196 Ibid.; S. Humphreys, 351–356, 360.

197 Runciman, *A History of the Crusades*, 3.307; Richard, 349–365.

198 Humphreys, 358–360.

199 Panchenko, "Razorenie sleniia."

200 Runciman, *A History of the Crusades*, 3.316–326; Briun, 2.493–509.

201 Runciman, *A History of the Crusades*, 3.319–20; Briun, 2.444–452.

202 For details, see Briun, 2.524–530.

203 Salibi, "The Maronites of Lebanon," 294–295; Salibi, "Maronite Historians," 63.

204 Irwin, 75; Runciman, *A History of the Crusades*, 3.403–407.

205 Jabre-Mouawad, "Un témoin melkite," 134–135; Kilpatrick, "Poetry on Political Events in the Mamluk and Early Ottoman Periods," 297–305.

206 On the Mamluk campaigns in Mount Lebanon, see Irwin, 79, 97, 101–102.

207 Bat Yeor, 56–59, 70–73, 75–81; Browne, 174–178; Meinardus, 12; Atiya, 97–98; Koraev, 44–45, 48–49.

208 Brett, "Population and Conversion," 25–30.

209 Panchenko, "Bulus al'-Khabis."

210 Swanson, 102–103; Irwin, 98–99.

211 For details, see Panchenko, "Podzhog Kaira 1321 g."

212 Irwin, 112–114; Swanson, 104.

213 Irwin, 141–142; T. K. Koraev, 48; Swanson, 101.

214 For details, see Panchenko, "Zabytaia katastrofa"; Panchenko, "V god Aleksandriii."

215 Dols, *The Black Death in the Middle East.*

216 Swanson, 119–120.

217 Browne, 178.

218 Reifenberg, 58, 99; Smilianskaia, 25.

219 On the disappearance of the settled population in the Syrian steppe in the thirteenth and fourteenth centuries, see Grabar, 8, 11, 161.

220 Reifenberg, 59.

221 Le Strange, 41.

222 Koraev, 47.

223 Nasrallah, *Histoire*, 3(2).50, 83.

224 MS Lattakia 28.

225 Nasrallah, *Histoire*, 3(2).99, 108–110; Panchenko, "Greki vs. Araby," 22–23; Panchenko, "Pravoslavnye vrachi na Arabskom Vostoke."

226 Korobeinikov, 4–5; Vryonis, 320.

227 Browne, 170–171.

228 Timur was a Turco-Mongol ruler who founded an empire broadly encompassing present-day Afghanistan, Iran, and other parts of Central Asia. Also known as Tamerlane he saw himself as an heir to the legacy of Genghis Khan.

229 Atiya, 276.

230 Browne, 172.

231 Korobeinikov, 9–10, 15.

232 Vryonis, 351–402; Korobeinikov, 9, 17–18.

233 On the extinction of Coptic monasteries and the reduction in the number of diocesan sees, see also Swanson, 125.

234 Jotischky, 85.

235 Frenkel, 112–113.

236 Sava Nemanjić, 3, 4, 17, 34, 37, 59; Agrefenii, 274–275; Ignaty Smol'nianin, 21–22; Zosima, 35–38; Daniel of Ephesus, 54–58; M. Sharon, 3.48–54; Felix Fabri, 33–35.

237 Sava Nemanjić, 3, 4, 35–36; Agrefenii, 275–276; Zosima, 35, 36; Frenkel, 114–115.

238 Frenkel, 113.

239 Nasrallah, *Histoire*, 3(2).82–87.

240 Hesychasm is a mystical movement, cultivated in the Orthodox monastic tradition and focused on the participation in the divine energy (the light of Tabor), which is active in the world. In fourteenth-century Byzantium, hesychasm acquired the traits of an ideological and political movement and played a prominent role in public life.

241 Tsagareli, 130, 193–240; Porphyry Uspenskii, *Kniga bytiia moego*, 8.47–48.

242 Sava Nemanjić, 36; Nasrallah, *Histoire*, 3(2). 88–89; Tsagareli, 222; Peristeris, 175–176.

243 MS Damascus 433; "Kratkii obzor sobraniia rukopisei," Part II, 14.

244 Rose, 243; Pahlitzsch, "Georgians and Greeks," 36–38.

245 Pahlitzsch, "Georgians and Greeks," 40–45; Müller and J. Pahlitzsch, 268–281.

246 Tsagareli, 97–106, 116–123.

247 Arkhim. Leonid, "Serbskaia inocheskaia obshchina," 42–53; Popović, 389–390, 400–406.

248 Runciman, *The Historic Role of Christian Arabs*, 12–13; Nasrallah, *Histoire*, 3(2).147.

249 Rose, 241.

250 Pahlitzsch, "Georgians and Greeks," 47.

251 Nasrallah, *Histoire*, 3(2).50–51.

252 Pahlitzsch, "Georgians and Greeks," 48.

253 Pahlitzsch, "Georgians and Greeks," 46–47; Nasrallah, *Histoire*, 3(2).52.

254 Maximus Simaius, 34–35; Murav'ev, *Istoriia*, 2.244–248; Nasrallah *Histoire*, 3(2).68–69.

255 Nicol, 291.

256 Papadopulo-Keramevs, iii–xi.

257 Troupeau, 147.

258 Zosima, 23.

259 Nasrallah, *Histoire*, 3(2).49.

260 Cheikho, 677.f.

261 K. A. Panchenko, "Greki vs. araby," 17–19.

262 Nasrallah, *Histoire*, 3(2).166–167, 171.

263 Briun, 2.214–218, 314–315, 371–374, 386–392.

264 Panchenko, "Evfimii I, patriarkh Antiokhiisii."

265 Nasrallah, "Chronologie, 1250–1500," 8–10.

266 Panchenko, "Dionisii I, patriarkh Antiokhiiskii."

267 Nasrallah, "Chronologie, 1250–1500," 10–11; Nasrallah, *HMLEM*, 3(2).107.

268 Gregory Palamas (c. 1296–1357)—an Athonite monk and later archbishop of Thessalonica, the spiritual leader of the hesychast movement.

269 Nasrallah, "Chronologie, 1250–1500," 13–18; Nasrallah, *Histoire*, 3(2).65–66.

270 Nasrallah, *Histoire*, 3(2).66–71.

271 Panchenko, "K istorii russko-vostochnykh sviazei," 5–20.

272 al-Qalqashandi, 11.393–395, 424–427.

273 Matveevskii, 261, 266.

274 Matveevskii, 375–381; Lebedev, 273–275; Nasrallah, *Histoire*, 3(2).59–62.

275 Nasrallah, *Histoire*, 3(2).58, 62.

276 Nasrallah, *Histoire,* 62, 148–149.

277 *Kratkii obzor sobraniia rukopisei,* 138; MS Lattakia 28; Nasrallah, *Histoire*, 3(2).148–149.

278 Nasrallah, *Histoire*, 3(2).58.

279 Panchenko "Miracles of Patriarch Yuwakim"; Panchenko, "Ispit' smertnoe zel'e."

280 Veselovskii, 14–33.

281 Karalevskij, "Antioche," col. 632; Nasrallah, *Histoire*, 3(2).72–73.

282 Nasrallah, *Histoire*, 3(2).73–74; Zanemonets, 86–100.

283 Nasrallah, *Histoire*, 3(2).79; Karalevskij, "Antioche," col. 632–634.

284 Kobeko, 272–275; Panchenko, "Patriarkh Ioakim," 229–234.

285 Nasrallah, *Histoire*, 3(2).79; Nasrallah, "Chronologie, 1250–1500," 34–35.

286 Panchenko, "Patriarkh Ioakim."

287 L. Eckenstein, 166; Porphyry Uspenskii, *Pervoe puteshestvie*, 140–141.

288 Panchenko, "Iakov II, patriarkh Ierusalimskii."

289 Nasrallah, *Histoire*, 3(2).76; Nasrallah, "Chronologie, 1250–1500," 34; Runciman, *The Great Church in Captivity*, 228.

290 Shawbak is located in the south of present-day Jordan at one of the highest elevations in that country.

291 Bakhit, 44–45.

292 Felix Fabri, 154–162; Frenkel, 115; K. A. Panchenko, "Greki vs. araby," 27; K. A. Panchenko, "'Temnyi vek'," 66–67.

293 Eckenstein, 162–163; A. Von Harff, 141; Nasrallah, *Histoire*, 3(2).85–86.

294 Ernst, 210–249.

295 Matveevskii, 369.

296 Zhuze, 486–492; Todt, "Notitia und Diozesen."

Glossary of Terms

Caliph—The successor to Muhammad as the ruler of the Islamic community.

Copts—A subethnicity composed of indigenous Egyptian Christians. Genetically, they trace back to the ancient Egyptians of the Pharaonic era; however, the Coptic identity and culture has nothing to do with the ancient Egyptian civilization. Their identity was formed in the first centuries AD under the influence of Christianity. In the fifth and sixth centuries, the Copts adopted the Monophysite confession and created their own ecclesiastical structure parallel to the Byzantine Orthodox Church. During the course of the tenth to the fourteenth centuries, they underwent a process of Arabization. The Coptic language survived only as a sacred language of worship. In the Ottoman era, they constituted about 10 percent of the population of Egypt.

Dhimmi (Arab. *ahl al-dhimma*, "the protected")—A non-Muslim living in Muslim lands and of an abject social status.

Diptychs—A list kept by each self-governing Orthodox Church of the heads of the other self-governing Orthodox churches that they are in communion with. These names are commemorated during church services when the chief celebrant is the head of a self-governing Orthodox Church.

Dragoman ("translator")—1. An official in the patriarchate in charge of relations with the secular Muslim authorities and in charge of organizing pilgrimages.

2. The grand dragoman of the Sublime Porte was a high-ranking official in the office of external relations of the Ottoman state.

Until the Greek uprising of 1821, those appointed to the post were Phanariot Greeks.

3. In the diplomatic practice of the nineteenth century, an official in a consulate or embassy who as a rule was locally born and who served as a mediator for a diplomatic representative.

Druze—An extreme Shiite sect, established in the eleventh century in the Lebanese mountains. The Druze doctrine combines elements of Islam, Christianity, Judaism, and Zoroastrianism. They are perceived as heretics by Sunni Muslims. In the Ottoman period, the Druze emirs and sheikhs controlled a significant part of Mount Lebanon.

Hajj (Arab.)—A pilgrimage. The term was applied equally to Muslim and Christian visitations to holy places. The person who has made the pilgrimage added the prefix "hajj" ("hajji") to his name.

Mamluks—Originally slaves who became soldiers under the 'Abbasid caliphate during the ninth century. By the thirteenth century, they had established a dynasty in Egypt that went on to conquer Palestine and Syria and maintain possession of them until the Ottoman conquest in the early sixteenth century.

Maronites—A subethnicity of Lebanese Christians who originally professed the Monothelete doctrine and then in the twelfth to sixteenth centuries were turned toward the union with Rome. The historical center of Maronite settlement was the northernmost foothills of the Lebanese mountains (Jubayl, Batroun, Jubbat Bsharri). In the Ottoman period, the Maronites colonized the more southern mountainous region of Lebanon (Keserwan and areas of the Chouf), and a large community of Maronites emerged in Aleppo. In contrast with the majority of other Middle Eastern Christians, the Maronites had their own military and political elite, a "feudal" aristocracy, which actively participated in the struggle for control of Mount Lebanon. The Druze Shihab dynasty, which dominated Lebanon from the eighteenth century until the first half of the nineteenth century, relied on the support of Maronite clans. In the middle of the eighteenth century, part of the Shihab clan converted to Maronite Christianity.

Monophysites (Greek: *mone physis* "one nature")—Adherents of a religious doctrine that postulates that after the Incarnation, Christ had one composite, divine-human nature. The radical form of this doctrine (eutychianism) emerged in the first half of the fifth century and was condemned at the Council of Chalcedon in 451 after which the Monophysites split from the dominant Orthodox Church of the Byzantine Empire and formed their own ecclesiastical bodies. The Armenian Apostolic Church, the Syriac Jacobite Church, Coptic, Ethiopic, and some other churches belong to the commonwealth of monophysite churches.

Monotheletes (Greek: *monos* "one single" and *thelema* "will")— Adherents of a religious doctrine adopted in the 630s by the Byzantine emperor Heraclius with the aim of reconciling the Orthodox and the Monophysites. Monotheletes recognize the presence of two natures in Christ, divine and human, and only one divine will. This confession was condemned at the Sixth Ecumenical Council. The adherents of Monotheletism in the Syro-Lebanese region formed their own church and later formed the subethnicity of the Maronites. In the twelfth century, the Maronite church accepted the union with Rome that had finally solidified by the sixteenth century.

Mulk (Arab.)—Privately owned property.

Nestorians—Adherents of a religious doctrine that formed in the beginning of the fifth century and professed the existence of two natures in Christ after the Incarnation, the divine and the human, with each one having its own hypostasis (concrete manifestation) and united in one person of Christ. After the condemnation of Nestorianism at the Council of Ephesus in 431, the Nestorians migrated from Byzantium to the Sasanian Empire, where their doctrine received support from the Christian communities of

Mesopotamia. At the end of the fifth century, they united to form the self-governing Church of the East.

Orthodox—Christian believers belonging to one of the local self-governing churches who maintained a continuity of belief and life from the time of the first Apostles. Orthodoxy was defined by St Athanasius of Alexandria (c. 293–373 AD) as "what Christ taught, the apostles preached, and the Fathers kept."

Sharia (Arab.)—The set of regulations in Islamic law.

Sheikh (Arab. *shaykh* "elder")—The head of a tribe or community; honorary title.

Syriac Jacobites, Jacobites—The community of Syriac Monophysites. They are named for the bishop Jacob Baradaeus, the spiritual leader of the Monophysites in the sixth century. In the Middle Ages, the Syriac Jacobite community was sizable and prosperous, but in the Ottoman period, it was considerably reduced and went into a deep decline. The core settlement of the Syriac Jacobites was the hilly region of Tur Abdin with its center in the city of Mardin on the watershed in the middle of the Tigris and Euphrates. Separate groups of Syriac Jacobites lived in Aleppo, Homs, and villages in central Syria.

Vizier (Arab. *wazir*)—The highest dignitary of the Ottoman Empire, a member of the apparatus of the central government with the rank of three-tailed pasha. Many provincial governors took on the title vizier. In European and Russian literature, it is often used as a synonym for the term *sadrazam* (grand vizier), the head of the apparatus of the central government.

Wali (Arab., Turk. *beylerbey*)—A deputy, provincial governor (of an eyalet or pashalik) with the title of pasha.

Maps

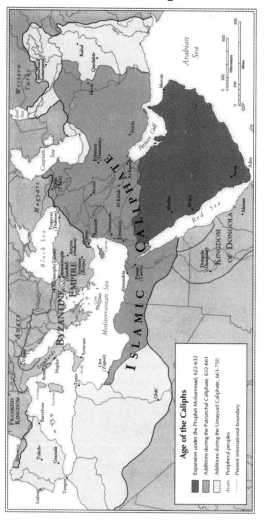

Age of the Caliphs

- Expansion under the Prophet Mohammad, 622-632
- Additions during the Patriarchal Caliphate, 632-661
- Additions during the Umayyad Caliphate, 661-750
- Asurs Peripheral peoples
- Present international boundary

The Arab conquests under the caliphs from 622 to 750. For the word "Patriarchal" in the legend read "Rightly Guided."

Source: United States. Central Intelligence Agency. "Age of the Caliphs." Map, 1993. Source: Norman B. Leventhal Map & Education Center, https://collections.leventhalmap.org/search/commonwealth:q524n615z

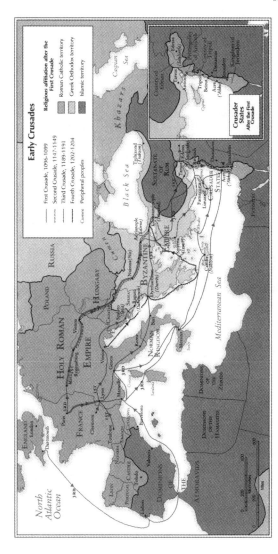

The era of the Crusades.

Source: United States. Central Intelligence Agency. "Early Crusades." Map, 1993. Source: Norman B. Leventhal Map & Education Center, https://collections.leventhalmap.org/search/commonwealth/qs24n6167

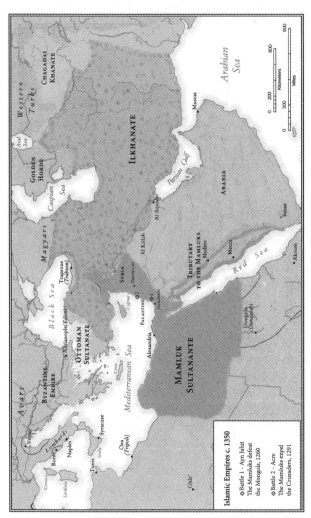

The Mamluk Sultanate in Egypt and the Levant circa 1350.

Design based on data from: Bonnie G. Smith, Marc Van De Mieroop, et al. *Crossroads and Cultures, Volume A: To 1300: A History of the World's Peoples* (Boston: Bedford/St Martin's, 2012) p. 496.

Works Cited

Manuscript Collections

Cheikho, Louis. "*Al-Makhtutat al-ʿarabiyya* fi khaznat kulliyyatina al-sharqiyya." *Al-Machreq* 7 (1904): 33–38, 73–79, 122–128, 276–283, 331–336, 487–490, 676–682, 1066–1072.

Damascus. *Al-Makhtutat al-ʿarabiyya* fi maktabat Batriyarkiyyat Antakiya wa-Saʾir al-Mashriq lil-Rum al-Urthudhuks. Beirut: Markaz al-Dirasat al-Urthudhuksi al-Antaki, 1998.

Kratkii obzor sobraniia rukopisei, prinadlezhavshego preosv. ep. Porfiriiu a nyne khraniashchegosia v Imperatorskoi Publichnoi biblioteke. St Petersburg: Tipografiia V. S. Balasheva, 1885.

Lattakia. "Makhtutat Abrashiyyat al-Ladhaqiyya." In *al-Makhtutat al-ʿArabiyya fi Abrashiyyat Hums wa-Hama wal-Ladhaqiyya lil-Rum al-Urthudhuks.* Beirut: Qism al-tawthiq wal-dirasat al-Antakiyya, Jamiʿat al-Balamand, 1994.

Troupeau, Gérard. *Catalogue des manuscrits arabes. Première partie. Manuscrits Chrétiens. Tome I.* Paris: Bibliothèque Nationale, 1972.

Primary Sources

Agrefenii. "Khozhenie arkhimandrita Agfeniia." In *Antologiia khozhenii russkikh puteshestvennikov XII-XV veka*, edited by E. I. Maleto. Moscow: Nauka, 2005.

Arculf. "The Travels of Bishop Arculf in the Holy Land." In *Early Travels in Palestine: Comprising the Narratives of Arculf, Willibald, Bernard, Saewulf, Sigurd, Benjamin of Tudela, Sir John Maundeville, De La Brocquière, and Maundrell*, edited by Thomas Wright, 1–12. New York: AMS Press, 1969.

Bernard the Wise. "The Voyage of Bernard the Wise." In *Early Travels in Palestine: Comprising the Narratives of Arculf, Willibald, Bernard, Saewulf, Sigurd, Benjamin of Tudela, Sir John Maundeville, De La Brocquière, and Maundrell*, edited by Thomas Wright, 23–31. New York: AMS Press, 1969.

Daniel of Ephesus. *Rasskaz i puteshestie po sviatym mestam Daniila mitropolita Efesskogo*. St Petersburg, 1904.

Daniil. *'Khozhenie' igumena Daniila v Sviatuiu zemliu v nach. XII v*. St Petersburg: Izdatel'stvo Olega Abyshko, 2007.

Ernst, Hans. *Die mamlukischen Sultansurkunden des Sinai-Klosters*. Wiesbaden: Otto Harrassowitz, 1960.

Eutychius of Alexandria. *Eutychii Patriarchae Alexandrini Annales*, edited by Louis Cheikho. 1–2 Vols. Paris: C. Poussielgue, 1906 and 1909.

Felix Fabri. *The Book of the Wanderings of Brother Felix Fabri*. 2 Vols. London: Committee of the Palestine Exploration Fund, 1893.

von Harff, Arnold. *The Pilgrimage of Arnold von Harff from Cologne, through Italy, Syria, Egypt, Arabia, Ethiopia, Nubia, Palestine, Turkey, France and Spain, which He Accomplished in the Years 1469 to 1499*. Nendeln, Liechtenstein: Kraus Reprint, 1967.

Ibn al-ʿAdim, Kamal al-Din. "Slivki, sniatye s istorii Khaleba." In *Iz istorii srednevekovoi Sirii: Sel'dzhukskii period*, edited by L. A. Semonova, 104–217. Moscow: Nauka, 1990.

Ignaty Smol'nianin. *Khozhdenie Ignatiia Smolnianina*. St Petersburg: Tipografiia V. Kirshbauma, 1887.

"Istoricheskoe skazanie o podvizhnichestve sviatogo velikomuchenika Ilii Novogo iz iliopolitov, postradavshchego v Damaske." *Sbornik palestinskoi i siriiskoi agiologii* 1 (1907): 49–68.

John Phocas. *Ioanna Foki skazanie vkratse o gorodakh i strankah ot Antiokhii do Ierusalima ... kontsa XII v*. St Petersbug: Tipografiia V. Kirshbauma, 1889.

Kuchuk-Ioannesov, Kh. "Pis'mo imperatora Ioanna Tsimiskhiia k armianskomu tsariu Ashotu III." *Khristianskii Vostok* 10 (1903): 91–101.

Matthew of Edessa. *Armenia and the Crusades: Tenth to Twelfth Centuries: The Chronicle of Matthew of Edessa*. Lanham, MD: University Press of America, 1993.

Maximus Simaius. "Istoriia Ierusalimskikh patriarkhov so vremen 6 vselenskogo sobora do 1810 g." In *Materialy dlia istorii Ierusalimskoi patriarkhii XVI-XIV v.*, edited by P. V. Bezobrazov, 1–130. 2 Vols. St Petersburg: Tipografiia V. Kirshbauma, 1904.

Michael the Syrian. *Chronique de Michel le Syrien*, edited by Jean-Baptiste Chabot. 3 Vols. Paris: Ernest Leroux, 1905.

Ieromonakh Mikhail. "Predislovie k Zhitiyu Ioanna Damaskina (o padenii Antiokhii 1084 g.)," translated into Russian by S. A. Moiseeva with a commentary by K. A. Panchenko. In *Antologiia literatury praoslavnykh arabov*, vol. 1, edited by K. A. Panchenko, 151–162. Moscow: Izdatel'stvo PSTGU, 2020.

Nicephorus Bryennius. *Istoricheskie zapiski Nikifora Vrienniia (976–1087)*. Moscow: Posev, 1997.

Palmer, Andrew et al. *The Seventh Century in the West-Syrian Chronicles*. Liverpool: Liverpool University Press, 1993.

Papadopulo-Keramevs, A. I. *Muchenichestvo shestidesiati novykh sviatykh muchenikov, postravdashikh vo Sviatom grade Khrista Boga nashego pod vladychestvom arabov*. St Petersbug: Pravoslavnyi Palestinskii Sbornik, 1892.

al-Qalqashandi, Abu al-ʿAbbas Ahmad. *Kitab subh al-aʿsha*. 11 Vols. Cairo, 1336/1918.

Sæwulf. "Puteshestvie Zevul'fa v Sviatuiu Zemliu 1102–1103 gg." In *Zhit'e i khozhden'e Daniila, Russkiya zemli igumena 1106–1108 g.* Part 2, 263–291. St Petersburg, 1885.

Sava Nemanjić. *Puteshestvie sv. Savvy, arkhiepiskopa Serbskogo*, edited by Archimandrite Leonid. St Petersburg, 1884.

Sharon, Moshe. *Corpus inscriptionum Arabicarum Palaestinae*, vol 3. Leiden: Brill, 2004.

"Skazanie o muchenichestve sviatykh ottsov, izbiennykh varvarami saratsinami v velikoi lavre prepodobnogo otsa nashego Savvy." *Sbornik palestinskoi i siriiskoi agiologii* 1 (1907): 1–48.

Theophanes the Confessor. *Letopis' vizantitsa Feofana ot Diokleti-ana do tsarei Mikhaila i syna ego Feofilakta*. Moscow: V Univ. tip. (M. Katkov), 1894.

Treiger, Alexander. "Unpublished Texts from the Arab Orthodox Tradition: On the Origin of the Term "Melkite" and the Destruction of the Meryamiyya Cathedral in Damascus." *Chronos* 29 (2014): 7–37.

Treiger, Alexander. "Unpublished Texts from the Arab Orthodox Tradition (2): Miracles of St. Eustratius of Mar Saba (written ca. 860)." *Chronos* 33 (2016): 7–20.

Treiger, Alexander. "Unpublished Texts from the Arab Orthodox Tradition (3): The Paterikon of the Palestinian Lavra of Mar Chariton." *Chronos* 38 (2019): 7–46.

Uspenskii, Porphyry. *Kniga bytiia moego*. 1–8 Vols. St Petersburg: Izd. Imp. akademii nauk, 1894–1902.

Uspenskii, Porphyry. *Pervoe puteshestvie v Sinaiskii monastyr' v 1845 g. arkhimandrita Porfiriia Uspenskogo*. St Petersburg: Tipografiia Imp. akademii nauk, 1856.

Uspenskii, Porphyry. *Vtoroe puteshestvie arkhimandrita Porfiriia Uspenskogo v Sinaiskii monastyr' v 1850 godu*. St Petersburg: Tipografiia morskago kadetskago korpusa, 1856.

Willibald. "The Travels of Willibald." In *Early Travels in Palestine: Comprising the Narratives of Arculf, Willibald, Bernard, Saewulf, Sigurd, Benjamin of Tudela, Sir John Maundeville, De La Brocquière, and Maundrell*, edited by Thomas Wright, 13–22. New York: AMS Press, 1969.

Yahya al-Antaki. *Eutychii Patriarchae Alexandrini Annales. Pars Posterior. Accedunt Annales Yahia Ibn Said Antiochensis*, edited by Louis Cheikho. Paris: C. Poussielgue, 1909.

Zosima. "Khozhdenie Zosimy v Tsar'grad, Afon i Palestinu," edited by N. I. Prokof'ev. *Voprosy Russkoi Literatury* 455 (1971): 12–42.

Secondary Sources

Atiya, Aziz. *A History of Eastern Christianity*. London: Methuen, 1968.

Bakhit, Muhammad Adnan. "The Christian Population of the Province of Damascus in the Sixteenth Century." In *Christians and Jews in the Ottoman Empire: The Functioning of a Plural Society Volume 2*, edited by Benjamin Braude and Bernard Lewis, 19–66. New York: Holmes and Meier, 1982.

Bartol'd, V. V. "Islam i melkity." In *Sochineniia*, 651–658. 6 Vols. Moscow: Izdatel'stvo vostochnoi literatury, 1966.

Bartol'd, V. V. "K voprosu o franko-musul'manskikh otnosheniiakh." *Khristianskii Vostok* 3 (1914): 263–296.

Bartol'd, V. V. "Karl Velikii i Kharun al-Rashid." In *Sochineniia*, 342–364. 6 Vols. Moscow: Izdatel'stvo vostochnoi literatury, 1966.

Bartol'd, V. V. "Khalif Omar II i protivorechivye izvestiia o ego lichnosti." In *Sochineniia*, 504–531. 6 Vols. Moscow: Izdatel'stvo vostochnoi literatury, 1966.

Bartol'd, V. V. "Review of Lektsii po istorii Vizantii by A. A. Vasil'ev." In *Sochineniia*, 575–594. 6 Vols. Moscow: Izdatel'stvo vostochnoi literatury, 1966.

Bat Yeor. *Zimmii: Evrei i khristiane pod vlastiu islama*. 2 Vols. Jerusalem: Biblioteka Aliia, 1991.

Belen'kaia, E. M. *"Leontii II."* In *Pravoslavnaia Entsiklopediia Volume 40*, 527–531.

Bisheh, Ghazi et al. *The Umayyads: The Rise of Islamic Art*. Amman: Museum with no Frontiers, 2000.

Boiko, K. A. *Arabskaia Istoricheskaia literatura v Egipte IX-X vv*. Moscow: Nauka, 1991.

Bol'shakov, O. G. *Istoriia Khalifata*, vol. 2. Moscow: Nauka, 1998.

Bol'shakov, O. G. "Vizantiia i Khalifat v VII-X vv." In *Vizantiia mezhdu Zapadom i Vostokom*, 354–379. St Petersburg: Aleteiia, 2001.

Borrut, Antoine and Fred Donner. "Introduction." In *Christians and Others in the Umayyad State*, edited by Antoine Borrut and Fred Donner, 1–10. Chicago, IL: The Oriental Institute of the University of Chicago, 2016.

Brett, Michael. "Al-Karaza al-Marqusiya. The Coptic Church in the Fatimid Empire." In *Egypt and Syria in the Fatimid, Ayyubid and Mamluk Eras IV: Proceedings of the 9th and 10th International Colloquium Organized at the Katholieke Universiteit Leuven in May 2000 and May 2001*, edited by Urbain Vermeulen and J. van Steenbergen, 33–60. Louvain: Peeters, 2005.

Brett, Michael. "Population and Conversion to Islam in Egypt in the Medieval Period." In *Egypt and Syria in the Fatimid, Ayyubid and Mamluk Eras IV: Proceedings of the 9th and 10th International Colloquium Organized at the Katholieke Universiteit Leuven in May 2000 and May 2001*, edited by Urbain Vermeulen and J. van Steenbergen, 1–32. Louvain: Peeters, 2005.

Briun, S. P. *Romen i franki v Antiokhii, Sirii i Kilikii*. Vols. 1–2. Moscow: Maska, 2015.

Brooks, E. W. "The Sources of Theophanes and the Syriac Chroniclers." *Byzantinische Zeitschrift* 15 (1906): 578–587.

Browne, Laurence E. *The Eclipse of Christianity in Asia from the Time of Muhammad till the Fourteenth Century*. New York: Fertig, 1967.

Burns, Ross. *Monuments of Syria: An Historical Guide*. New York: I.B. Tauris, 199.

Dmitrievskii, A. A. "Drevneishie patriarshie Tikikony ierusalimskii (sviatogrobskii) i konstantinopolskii (Velikoi tserkvi). Gl. 2." *Trudy Kievskoi Dukhovnoi Akademii* (January 1901): 34–86.

Dols, Michael W. *The Black Death in the Middle East*. Princeton, NJ: Princeton University Press, 1977.

Eckenstein, Lina. *A History of Sinai*. London: Society for Promoting Christian Knowledge, 1921.

Encyclopedia of Archaeological Excavations in the Holy Land, edited by Michael Avi-Yonah and Ephraim Stern. 4 Vols. Oxford: Oxford University Press, 1975–1978.

Fargues, Philippe. "The Arab Christians of the Middle East: A Demographic Perspective." In *Christian Communities in the Arab Middle East: The Challenge of the Future*, edited by Andrea Pacini, 48–66. Oxford: Clarendon Press, 1998.

Fil'shtinskii, I. M. *Istoriia arabov i khalifata (750–1517 gg.)*. Moscow: Muravei - Gaid, 1999.

Finkelstein, Israel. "Byzantine Monastic Remains in Southern Sinai." *Dumbarton Oaks Papers* 39 (1985): 39–79.

Frenkel, Yehoshu'a. "Mar Saba during the Mamluk and Ottoman Periods." In *The Sabaite Heritage in the Orthodox Church from the Fifth Century to the Present*, edited by Joseph Patrich, 111–116. Leuven: Peeters, 2001.

Grabar, Oleg. *City in the Desert: Qasr al-Hayr East: An Account of the Excavations Carried Out at Qasr al-Hayr East*. Cambridge, MA: Harvard University Press, 1978.

Graf, Georg. *Geschichte der christlichen arabischen Literatur*, vol. 3. Vatican City: Biblioteca Apostolica Vaticana, 1949.

Griffith, Sidney H. "Anthony David of Bagdad, Scribe and Monk of Mar Saba: Arabic in the Monasteries of Palestine." In *Arabic Christianity in the Monasteries of Ninth-Century Palestine*. Aldershot: Variorum, 1992, Essay XI, 7–19.

Griffith, Sidney H. "The Arabic Account of 'Abd al-Masih an-Nagrani al-Ghassani." In *Arabic Christianity in the Monasteries of Ninth-Century Palestine*. Aldershot: Variorum, 1992, Essay X, 331–374.

Griffith, Sidney H. "Greek into Arabic: Life and Letters in the Monasteries of Palestine in the Ninth Century: The Example of the *Summa Theologica Arabica*." In *Arabic Christianity in the Monasteries of Ninth-Century Palestine*. Aldershot: Variorum, 1992, Essay VIII, 117–138.

Griffith, Sidney H. "The Life of Theodore of Edessa: History, Hagiography and Religious Aplogetics in Mar Saba Monastery in Early 'Abbasid Times." In *The Sabaite Heritage in the Orthodox*

Church from the Fifth Century to the Present, edited by Joseph Patrich, 147–169. Leuven: Peeters, 2001.

Griffith, Sidney H. "The Manṣūr Family and Saint John of Damascus: Christians and Muslims in Umayyad Times." In *Christians and Others in the Umayyad State*, edited by Antoine Borrut and Fred Donner, 29–52. Chicago, IL: The Oriental Institute of the University of Chicago, 2016.

Griffith, Sidney H. "The Monks of Palestine and the Growth of Christian Literature in Arabic." *The Muslim World* 78 (1988): 1–28.

Grumel, Venance. "La Chronologie des patriarches Grecs de Jérusalem au XIIIe siècle." *Revue des Etudes Byzantines* 20 (1962): 197–201.

Hitti, Philip. *History of Syria: Including Lebanon and Palestine.* London: Macmillan, 1951.

Hiyari, Mustafa. "Crusader Jerusalem 1099–1187 AD." In *Jerusalem in History*, edited by Kamil Jamil Asali, 130–176. Brooklyn, NY: Olive Branch Press, 1990.

Humphreys, Stephen. *Muʿawiya ibn Abi Sufyan: From Arabia to Empire.* Oxford: Oneworld, 2006.

Irwin, Robert. *The Middle East in the Middle Ages: The Early Mamluk Sultanate 1250–1382.* London: Croom Helm, 1986.

Ivanov, N. A. *Programa kursa "Istoriia arabskikh stran."* Moscow, 1993.

Jabre-Mouawad, Ray. "Un témoin melkite de la prise de Tripoli par les mameluks (17 avril 1287)." In *Studies on the Christian Arabic Heritage: In Honour of Father Prof. Dr. Samir Khalil Samir*, edited by Rifat Ebeid and Herman Teule, 134–135. Leuven: Peeters, 2004.

Jotischky, Andrew. "Greek Orthodox and Latin Monasticism around Mar Saba under Crusader Rule." In *The Sabaite Heritage in the Orthodox Church from the Fifth Century to the Present*, edited by Joseph Patrich, 85–96. Leuven: Peeters, 2001.

Karalevskij, Cyrille. *Dictionairre d'histoire et de géographie ecclésiastiques*, s.v. "Antioche." 3 Vols. Paris: Letouzet et Ané, 1937. Cols. 1399–1405.

Kekelidze, K. "Gruzinskaia versiia arabskogo Zhitiia sv. Ioanna Damaskina." *Khristianskii Vostok* 3 (1914): 99–174.

Kilpatrick, Hilary. "Poetry on Political Events in the Mamluk and Early Ottoman Periods." In *A Festschrift for Nadia Anghelescu*, edited by Andrei Avram, Anca Focşeneanu and Gheorghe Grigore, 297–305. Bucharest: Editura Universității din București, 2011.

Kobeko, D. F. "Razreshitel'nye gramoty ierusalimskikh patriarkhov." *Zhurnal ministerstva narodnogo proveshcheniia* (June 1896): 270–279.

Koraev, T. K. "Musul'mansko-khristianskie otnosheniia v Egipte i Sirii epokhi mongolo-mamliukskikh voin (vtoraia polovina XIII-pervaia polovina XIV v.)." *Vestnik Moskovskogo universiteta* 4 (2005): 37–51.

Korobeinikov, Dimitri. "Orthodox Communities in Eastern Anatolia in the Thirteenth to Fourteenth Centuries. Part 2: The Time of Troubles." *Al-Masaq* 17 (2005): 1–29.

Krachkovskii, I. Iu. "Arabskaia geograficheskaia literatura." In *Izbrannye sochineniia*. 4 Vols. Moscow: Izdatel'stvo akademii nauk SSSR, 1957.

Krivov, M. V. "Araby-khristiane v Antiokhii X-XI vv." In *Traditsii i nasledie Khristianskogo Vostoka*, edited by D. E. Afinogenov and A. V. Murav'ev, 247–255. Moscow: Indrik, 1996.

Krivov, M. V. "Otnoshenie siriiskikh monofizitov k arabskomu zavoevaniiu." *Vizantiiskii Vremennik* 55 (1994): 95–103.

Kulakovskii, Yu. A. *Istoriia Vizantii*. 3 Vols. St Petersburg: Aleteiia, 1996.

Kuzenkov, P. V. and K. A. Panchenko. "'Krivye Paskhi' i Blagodatnyi ogon v istoricheskoi retrospektive." *Vestnik MGU, Ser. 13 Vostokovedenie* 4 (2006): 1–29.

Le Strange, Guy. *Palestine under the Moslems: A Description of Syria and the Holy Land from AD 650–1500*. Beirut: Khayats, 1965.

Lebedev, A. P. *Istoriia greko-vostochnoi tserkvi pod vlastiu turok: ot padaniia Konstantinopolia (1453 g.) do nastoiashchego vremeni*. 1–2 Vols. Sergiev Posad: Tipografiia A. N. Snegirevoi, 1896–1901.

Lev, Yaacov. *State and Society in Fatimid Egypt*. Leiden: Brill, 1991.

Leonid, Arkhim. "Serbskaia inocheskaia obshchina v Palestine." *Chteniia v imperatorskom obshchestve istorii i drevnostei rossiskikh 3* (1867): 42–65.

Leonid, Arkim. "Tri stati k russkomu palestinovedeniiu." *Pravoslavnyi Palestinskii Sbornik* 6, No. 1 (1889).

Levi-Rubin, Milka. "'Umar II's *ghiyār* Edict: Between Ideology and Practice." In *Christians and Others in the Umayyad State*, edited by Antoine Borrut and Fred Donner, 157–172. Chicago, IL: The Oriental Institute of the University of Chicago, 2016.

Loparev, Kh. M. "Vizantiiskie zhitie sviatykh VIII–IX vv." *Vizantiiskii Vremennik* 17 (1911): 1–223; 18 (1911): 1–147; 19 (1912): 1–151.

MacAdam, Henry Innes. "Settlements and Settlement Patterns in Northern and Central Transjordania, ca 550–750." In *The Byzantine and Early Islamic Near East: Land Use and Settlement Patterns*, edited by Averil Cameron and G. R. D. King, 49–94. Princeton: Darwin Press, 1994.

Matveevskii. "Ocherk istorii Aleksandriiskoi tserkvi so vremen Khalkidonskogo sobora." *Khristianskoe chtenie* (1856): 188–271, 358–419.

Mednikov, N. A. *Palestina ot zavoevaniia ee arabami do krestovykh pokhodov*. 1–2 Vols. St Petersburg: Izdat'elstvo Imp. pravoslavnago pelstinskago obshchestva, 1897–1903.

Meinardus, Otto. "Coptic Christianity Past and Present." In *Christian Egypt: Coptic Art and Monuments through Two Millennia*, edited by Massimo Capuani, 8–20. Cairo: American University of Cairo Press, 2002.

Mets, A. *Musul'manskii renessans*. Moscow: Nauka, 1973.

Moiseeva, S. A. and K. A. Panchenko. *Pravoslavnaia entsiklopediia*, s. v. "Orest, patriarkh Ierusalimskii." 53 Vols. Moscow: Tserkovno-nauchnii tsentr "Pravoslavnaia Entsiklopediia," 2019. 172–173.

Moosa, Matti. *The Maronites in History*. Syracuse, NY: Syracuse University Press, 1986.

Müller, Christian and Johannes Pahlitzsch. "Sultan Baybars I and the Georgians in Light of New Documents, Related to the Monastery of the Holy Cross in Jerusalem." *Arabica* 51 (2004): 258–290.

Murav'ev, A. N. *Istoriia sviatago grada Ierusalima, ot vremen apostol'skikh do nashikh.* 1–2 Vols. St Petersburg: V Tip. III. otdel. sobstv. E.I.V. kantseliarii, 1844.

Nasrallah. *Histoire du mouvement littéraire dans l'Eglise melchite du Ve au XXe siècle: Contribution à l'étude de la littérature arabe chrétienne.* 2.1–4.2 Vols. Louvain: Peeters, 1979–1989.

Nasrallah, Joseph. *Chronologie des patriarches melchites d'Antioche de 1250 à 1500.* Jerusalem, 1959.

Neale, John Mason. *A History of the Holy Eastern Church: The Patriarchate of Antioch.* London: Rivingtons, 1873.

Nicol, Donald M. "The Confessions of a Bogus Patriarch: Paul Tagaris Palaiologos, Orthodox Patriarch of Jerusalem and Catholic Patriarch of Constantinople in the Fourteenth Century." *Journal of Ecclesiastical History* 21 (1970): 289–299.

Pahlitzsch, Johannes. "Athanasios II, a Greek Orthodox Patriarch of Jerusalem (c. 1231–1244)." In *Autour de la première Croisade: Actes du colloque de la Society for the study of the Crusades and the Latin East, Clermont-Ferrand, 22–35 juin 1995,* edited by Michel Balard, 465–474. Paris: Publications de la Sorbonne, 1994.

Pahlitzsch, Johannes. "Georgians and Greeks in Jerusalem (1099–1310)." In *East and West in the Crusader States: Context, Contacts, Confrontations. III, Acts of the Congress Held at Hernen Castle in September 2000,* edited by Krijna Cigaar and Herman Teule, 35–52. Leuven: Peeters, 2003.

Panchenko, Constantin. "Miracles of Patriarch Yuwakim of Alexandria (1486–1567): An Attempt at a Historical Analysis." *Parole de l'Orient* 42 (2016): 289–404.

Panchenko, K. A. "Antiokhiiskii patriarkh Khristofor (um. 967 g.): lichnost' i epokha." In *XIV Ezhegodnaia bogoslovskaia konferentsiia PSTBI: Materialy,* 216–234. Moscow: Pravoslavnyi Sviato-Tikhonskii Bogoslovskii institut, 2005.

Panchenko, K. A. "Bulus al'-Khabis, koptskii novomuchenik XIII v.: sud'ba na fone epokhi." *Vestnik PSTGU, Ser. III. Filologiia* 45, No. 5 (2015): 61–69.

Panchenko, K. A. "Greki vs. Araby v Ierusalimskoi tserkvi XIII-XVIII vv." In *Meyeriana: Sbornik statei, posviashchennyi 70-letiiu M. S. Meiera*, 7–50. 2 Vols. Moscow: Institut stran azii i afrikii pri MGU, 2006.

Panchenko, K. A. "Ispit' smertnoe zel'e: Aleksandriiskii patriarkh Ioakim (1448–1576) mezhdu eposom I istoriei." *Khristianstvo na Blizhem vostoke. Istoricheskii Vestnik* 20 (2017): 136–163.

Panchenko, K. A. "K istorii pravoslavnogo letopisaniia v Khalifate (Istochniki khroniki Agapiia Manbadzhskogo)." *Vizantiiskii Vremennik* 60 (2001): 109–120.

Panchenko, K. A. "K istorii russko-vostochnykh sviazei 70-x gg. XIV v. O datirovke i obstoiatel'stvakh palomnichestva arkhimandrita Agrefeniia i pervogo priezda na Rus' blizhnevostochnykh mitropolitov." *Kapterevskie chteniia* 7 (2009): 5–20.

Panchenko, K. A. "Koptskii bunt: k analizu bashmurskikh vosstanii VIII-IX vv." *Vestnik PSTGU, Ser. III. Filologiia* 49, No. 4 (2016): 63–47.

Panchenko, K. A. "Kosta ibn Luka (830–912) i ego mesto v arabo-khristianskoi istoriografii." *Pravoslavnyi Palestinskii Sbornik* 100 (2003): 153–163.

Panchenko, K. A. "Patriarkh Ioakim mezhdu Kairom, Rimom i Moskvoi: K istorii russko-palestinskikh kontaktov XV v." In *Russkaia Palestina: Rossiia v sviatoi zemle*, edited by E. I. Zelenev, 228–239. St Petersburg: Izdatel'skii dom SPbGU, 2010.

Panchenko, K. A. "Podzhog Kaira 1321 g. i problema khristianskogo terrorizma v Mamliukskom gosudarstve." *Vestnik PTGSU, Ser. III. Filologiia* 4 No. 26 (2011): 96–124.

Panchenko, K. A. *Pravoslavnaia Entsiklopediia*, s.v. "Dionisii I, patriarkh Antiokhiiskii." 15 Vols. Moscow: Tserkovno-nauchnii tsentr "Pravoslavnaia Entsiklopediia," 2012. 308.

Panchenko, K. A. *Pravoslavnaia Entsiklopediia*, s.v. "Evfimii I, patriarkh Antiokhiiskii." 17 Vols. Moscow: Tserkovno-nauchnii tsentr "Pravoslavnaia Entsiklopediia," 2013. 425.

Panchenko, K. A. *Pravoslavnaia entsiklopediia*, s. v. "Iakov II, patri-arkh Ierusalimskii." 20 Vols. Moscow: Tserkovno-nauchnii tsentr "Pravoslavnaia Entsiklopediia," 2014. 514.

Panchenko, K. A. *Pravoslavnaia entsiklopediia*, s. v. "Nikolai I, patri-arkh aleksandriiskii." 50 Vols. Moscow: Tserkovno-nauchnii tsentr "Pravoslavnaia Entsiklopediia," 2014. 380–381.

Panchenko, K. A. "Pravoslavnye vrachi na Arabskom Vostoke." *Vestnik PSTGU, Ser. III. Filologiia* 35, No. 5 (2013): 59–75.

Panchenko, K.A. "Razorenie seleniia kara sultanom Beibarsom v 1266 g. Istoricheskii kontekst." *Vestnik PSTGU, Ser. III. Filologiia* 29, No. 3 (2012): 32–45.

Panchenko, K. A. "Razrushenie damasskoi cerkvi Mart Mariam v 924 g. Svidetel'stvo ochevidtsa." *Simvol* 61 (2012): 339–356.

Panchenko, K. A. "Rod Ioanna Damaskina i stanovlenie khristian-skoi elity v khalifate." *Vestnik MGU, Ser. 13. Vostokovedenie* (2002): 88–99.

Panchenko, K. A. "'Temnyi vek' palestinskogo monashestva: upadok i vozrozhdenie blishnevostochnykh monastyrei na rubezhe mam-liukskoi i osmanskoi epokh." *Vestnik PSTGU, Ser. III. Filologiia* 57, No. 4 (2018): 66–67.

Panchenko, K. A. "'V god Aleksandriii' K istorii mamliuksogo goneniia na khristian posle Aleksandriiskogo Krestovogo poxoda 1365 g." *Vestnik tserkovnoi istorii* 45–46, No. 1–2 (2017): 127–136.

Panchenko, K. A. "Vospriiatie istoricheskogo protsessa arabo-khristianskimi khronistami." In *Religii stran Azii i Afrikii: istoriia i sovremennost': Nauchnaia konferentsiia Lomonosovskie chteniia. Aprel' 2001. Tezisy dokladov*, 82–86. Moscow: Institut stran azii i afrikii pri MGU, 2002.

Panchenko, K. A. "Zabytaia katastrofa: k rekonstruktsii posledstvii Aleksandriiskogo krestovogo pokhoda 1365 g. na Khristianskom Vostoke." In *Pravoslavnye Araby: put' cherez veka*, edited by K. A. Panchenko, 202–219. Moscow: Izdatel'stvo PSTGU, 2013.

Peristeris, Aristarchos. "Literary and Scribal Activities at the Monas-tery of Mar Saba." In *The Sabaite Heritage in the Orthodox Church from the Fifth Century to the Present*, edited by Joseph Patrich, 171–177. Leuven: Peeters, 2001.

Piccirilo, Michele. "The Christians in Palestine during a Time of Transition: 7th–9th Centuries." In *The Christian Heritage in the Holy Land*, edited by Anthony O'Mahoney, 47–56. London: Scorpion Cavendish, 1995.

Plank, P. "Pravoslavnye khristiane Sv. Zemli vo vremena krestovykh pokhodov (1099–1197)." *Al'fa i Omega* 4, No. 26 (2000): 180–191.

Popov, Aleksandr. *Latinskaia ierusalimskaia patriarkhiia epokhi krestonostev*. St Petersburg: Pechatnia S. P. Iakovleva, 1903.

Popović, Svetlana. "Sabaite Influences on the Church in Medieval Serbia." In *The Sabaite Heritage in the Orthodox Church from the Fifth Century to the Present*, edited by Joseph Patrich, 385–407. Leuven: Peeters, 2001.

Potulov, V. "Maronitskaia tserkov' v V-IX vv." *Soobshcheniia Imperatorskago Pravoslavnago Palestinskago Obshchestva* 23 (1912): 32–52.

Reifenberg, Adolf. *The Struggle between the Desert and the Sown: Rise and Fall of Agriculture in the Levant*. Jerusalem: Publication Department of the Jewish Agency, 1956.

Richard, Jean. *Latino-Ierusalimskoe korolevstvo*. St Petersburg: Evrasia, 2002.

Robinson, Chase F. *Empire and Elites after the Muslim Conquest: The Transformation of the Northern Mesopotamia*. Cambridge: Cambridge University Press, 2000.

Rose, Richard B. "The Native Christians of Jerusalem, 1187–1260." In *The Horns of Hattin: Proceedings of the Second Conference of the Society for the Study of the Crusades and the Latin East, Jerusalem and Haifa, 2–6 July, 1987*, edited by Benjamin Z. Kedar, 239–249. London: Variorum, 1992.

Runciman, *The Historic Role of Christian Arabs of Palestine*. London: Harlow, Longmans, 1970.

Runciman, Steven. *The Great Church in Captivity*. Cambridge: Cambridge University Press, 1968.

Runciman, Steven. *A History of the Crusades*, 1–3 Vols. Cambridge: Cambridge University Press, 1968–1975.

Runciman, Steven. *Vostochnaia skhizma: Vizantiiskaia teokratiia*. Moscow: Nauka, 1998.

Salibi, Kamal. *Maronite Historians of Medieval Lebanon*. Beirut: American University of Beirut Faculty of Arts and Sciences, 1959.

Salibi, Kamal. "The Maronites of Lebanon under Frankish and Mamluk Rule (1099–1516)." *Arabica* 4 (1957): 288–303.

Sanders, Paula A. "The Fāṭimid State, 969–1171." In *The Cambridge History of Egypt Volume One: Islamic Egypt, 640–1517*, edited by Carl F. Petry, 151–174. Cambridge: Cambridge University Press, 1998.

Shick, Robert. "Archaeological Sources for the History of Palestine: Palestine in the Early Islamic Period: Luxuriant Legacy." *Near Eastern Archaeology* 61 (1998): 74–108.

Smilianskaia, I. M. *Sotsial'no-ekonomicheskaia struktura stran Blizhnego Vostoka na rubezhe Novogo vremeni*. Moscow: Nauka, 1979.

Swanson, Mark. "The Christian al-Maʿmun Tradition." In *Christians at the Heart of Islamic Rule: Church Life and Scholarship in ʿAbbasid Iraq*, edited by David Thomas, 63–92. Leiden: Brill, 2003.

Todt, Klaus-Peter. "Notitia und Diozesen des griechisch-orthodoxen Patriarchates von Antiocheia im 10. und 11. Jarhundert." *Orthodoxes Forum* 9 (1995): 173–185.

Todt, Klaus-Peter. *Region und griechisch-orthodoxes Patriarchat von Antiocheia im mittelbyzantinischer Zeit un im Zeitalter der Kreuzzüge (969–1204)*. Wiesbaden, 1998.

Tsagareli, A. *Pamiatniki gruzinskoi strany v Sviatoi zemle i na Sinae*. St Petersburg, 1888.

Uspenskii, F. I. *Istoriia Vizantiiskoi Imperii*. 1–3 Vols. Moscow: Mysl, 1996–1997.

Veselovskii, A. N. "K skazanniiu o prenii zhidov s khristianami." In *Zametki po literature i narodnoi slovestnosti*, 14–33. St Petersburg: Tip. Imp. Akademii Nauk, 1883.

Vryonis, Speros. *The Decline of Medieval Hellenism in Asia Minor and the Process of Islamization from the Eleventh through the Fifteenth Century*. Berkeley, CA: University of California Press, 1971.

Whitcomb, Donald. "Notes for an Archaeology of Muʿāwiya: Material Culture in the Transitional Period of Believers." In *Christians and Others in the Umayyad State,* edited by Antoine Borrut and Fred Donner, 11–28. Chicago, IL: The Oriental Institute of the University of Chicago, 2016.

Wilfong, Terry G. "The non-Muslim Communities: Christian Communities." In *The Cambridge History of Egypt Volume One: Islamic Egypt, 640–1517*, edited by Carl F. Petry, 175–197. Cambridge: Cambridge University Press, 1998.

Yarbrough, Luke. "Did ʿUmar b. ʿAbd al-ʿAzīz Issue an Edict Concerning Non-Muslim Officials?." In *Christians and Others in the Umayyad State*, edited by Antoine Borrut and Fred Donner, 173–206. Chicago, IL: The Oriental Institute of the University of Chicago, 2016.

Zanemonets, A. V. *Gennadii Skholarii, patriarkh Konstantinopolskii (1454–1456 g.)*. Moscow: Bibleisko-bogoslovskii Institut sv. Apostola Andreia, 2010.

Zayat, Habib. "Vie du patriarche melkite d'Antioche Christophore (d. 967) par le protospathaire Ibrahim b. Yuhanna. Document inédit du Xe siècle." *Proche-Orient Chrétien* 2 (1952): 11–38, 333–366.

Zeyadeh, Ali. "Settlement Patterns, An Archaeological Perspective: Case Studies from Northern Palestine and Jordan." In *In The Byzantine and Early Islamic Near East: Land Use and Settlement Patterns*, edited by Averil Cameron and G. R. D. King, 117–132. Princeton, NJ: Darwin Press, 1994.

Zhuze, P. "Eparkhii Antiokhiiskoi tserkvi." *Soobscheniia Imperatorskogo Pravoslavnago Palestinskago Obschestva* 22 (1911): 481–498.

Subject Index